studysync®

Reading & Writing Companion

Past and Present

What makes you, you?

studysync.com

Send all inquiries to:
BookheadEd Learning, LLC
610 Daniel Young Drive
Sonoma, CA 95476

ISBN 978-1-94-469586-6

7 8 9 SKY 24 23 22

B

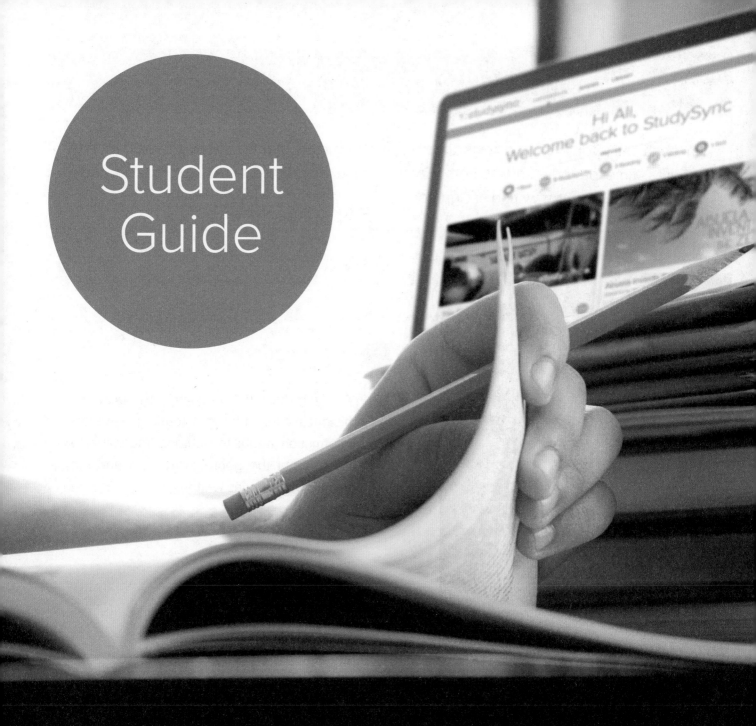

Student Guide

Getting Started

Welcome to the StudySync Reading & Writing Companion! In this book, you will find a collection of readings based on the theme of the unit you are studying. As you work through the readings, you will be asked to answer questions and perform a variety of tasks designed to help you closely analyze and understand each text selection. Read on for an explanation of each

Close Reading and Writing Routine

In each unit, you will read texts that share a common theme, despite their different genres, time periods, and authors. Each reading encourages a closer look through questions and a short writing assignment.

1 Introduction

An Introduction to each text provides historical context for your reading as well as information about the author. You will also learn about the genre of the text and the year in which it was written.

2 Notes

Many times, while working through the activities after each text, you will be asked to **annotate** or **make annotations** about what you are reading. This means that you should highlight or underline words in the text and use the "Notes" column to make comments or jot down any questions you have. You may also want to note any unfamiliar vocabulary words here.

You will also see sample student annotations to go along with the Skill lesson for that text.

Reading & Writing Companion

③ First Read

During your first reading of each selection, you should just try to get a general idea of the content and message of the reading. Don't worry if there are parts you don't understand or words that are unfamiliar to you. You'll have an opportunity later to dive deeper into the text.

④ Think Questions

These questions will ask you to start thinking critically about the text, asking specific questions about its purpose, and making connections to your prior knowledge and reading experiences. To answer these questions, you should go back to the text and draw upon specific evidence to support your responses. You will also begin to explore some of the more challenging vocabulary words in the selection.

⑤ Skills

Each Skill includes two parts: Checklist and Your Turn. In the Checklist, you will learn the process for analyzing the text. The model student annotations in the text provide examples of how you might make your own notes following the instructions in the Checklist. In the Your Turn, you will use those same instructions to practice the skill.

---

③ First Read

Read "The Tell-Tale Heart." After you read, complete the Think Questions below.

④ THINK QUESTIONS

1. Write two or three sentences explaining how the narrator feels about the old man and why he decides to murder him.

2. Does the narrator seem trustworthy as he gives his account of the events in the story? Cite evidence from the text to explain your opinions.

3. What sound does the narrator hear at the end of the story that causes him to confess to the murder? Provide evidence to support your inference.

4. Find the word **sufficient** in paragraph 3 of "The Tell-Tale Heart." Use context clues in the surrounding sentences, as well as the sentence in which the word appears, to determine the word's meaning. Write your definition here and identify clues that helped you figure out its meaning.

5. Use context clues to determine the meaning of **sagacity** as it is used in paragraph 4 of "The Tell-Tale Heart." Write your definition here and identify clues that helped you figure out its meaning. Then check the meaning in a dictionary.

---

⑤ Skill:
Language, Style, and Audience

Use the Checklist to analyze Language, Style, and Audience in "The Tell-Tale Heart." Refer to the sample student annotations about Language, Style, and Audience in the text.

••• CHECKLIST FOR LANGUAGE, STYLE, AND AUDIENCE

In order to determine an author's style, do the following:

✓ identify and define any unfamiliar words or phrases

✓ use context, including the meanings of surrounding words and phrases

✓ note possible reactions to the author's word choice

✓ examine your reaction to the author's word choice

✓ identify any analogies, or comparisons in which one part of the comparison helps explain the other

To analyze the impact of specific word choice on meaning and tone, ask the following questions:

✓ How did your understanding of the language change during your analysis?

✓ How do the writer's word choices impact or create meaning in the text?

✓ How do the writer's word choices impact or create a specific tone in the text?

✓ How could various audiences interpret this language? What different possible emotional responses can you list?

✓ What analogies do you see? Where might an analogy have clarified meaning or created a specific tone?

⟳ YOUR TURN

1. What effect do the punctuation choices in paragraphs 9 and 10 have on the tone?

    ○ A. The dashes and exclamation marks reveal that the narrator is losing control.
    ○ B. The italics make it clear that the narrator's words aren't to be trusted.
    ○ C. The semicolons introduce a formal tone into an informal speech.
    ○ D. The frequent questions reveal the narrator's attempt to engage the reader.

2. Which phrase from the passage most clearly suggests the narrator's disturbed mental state at the end of the story?

    ○ A. "but I talked more fluently"
    ○ B. "Why would they not be gone?"
    ○ C. "It grew louder—louder—louder!"
    ○ D. "And still the men chatted pleasantly"

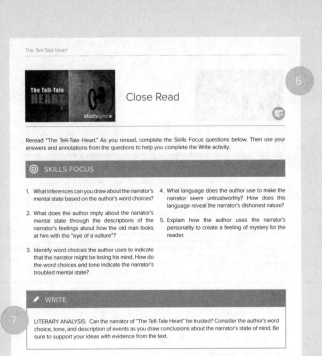

Close Read

studysync

Reread "The Tell-Tale Heart." As you reread, complete the Skills Focus questions below. Then use your answers and annotations from the questions to help you complete the Write activity.

SKILLS FOCUS

1. What inferences can you draw about the narrator's mental state based on the author's word choices?

2. What does the author imply about the narrator's mental state through the descriptions of the narrator's feelings about how the old man looks at him with the "eye of a vulture"?

3. Identify word choices the author uses to indicate that the narrator might be losing his mind. How do the word choices and tone indicate the narrator's troubled mental state?

4. What language does the author use to make the narrator seem untrustworthy? How does this language reveal the narrator's dishonest nature?

5. Explain how the author uses the narrator's personality to create a feeling of mystery for the reader.

WRITE

LITERARY ANALYSIS: Can the narrator of "The Tell-Tale Heart" be trusted? Consider the author's word choice, tone, and description of events as you draw conclusions about the narrator's state of mind. Be sure to support your ideas with evidence from the text.

Inside the House

DRAMA

Introduction

❝ "Inside the House" tells the story of two teenage siblings who spend a stormy night alone telling scary stories. In this scene from the play, Cristina and Fernando learn just how scary a story can be when their real life starts to match a tale they've told. The author uses dialogue, sound effects, and foreshadowing to build suspense.

VOCABULARY

predictable
easily guessed or expected

anxious
nervous or afraid

sarcastic
meaning the opposite of what is said to express humor, irritation, or meanness

embarrassed
feeling foolish or ashamed

Close Read & Skills Focus

After you have completed the First Read, you will be asked to go back and read the text more closely and critically. Before you begin your Close Read, you should read through the Skills Focus to get an idea of the concepts you will want to focus on during your second reading. You should work through the Skills Focus by making annotations, highlighting important concepts, and writing notes or questions in the "Notes" column. Depending on instructions from your teacher, you may need to respond online or use a separate piece of paper to start expanding on your thoughts and ideas.

Write

Your study of each selection will end with a writing assignment. For this assignment, you should use your notes, annotations, personal ideas, and answers to both the Think and Skills Focus Questions. Be sure to read the prompt carefully and address each part of it in your writing.

English Language Learner

The English Language Learner texts focus on improving language proficiency. You will practice learning strategies and skills in individual and group activities to become better readers, writers, and speakers.

Extended Writing Project and Grammar

This is your opportunity to use genre characteristics and craft to compose meaningful, longer written works exploring the theme of each unit. You will draw information from your readings, research, and own life experiences to complete the assignment.

1 Writing Project

After you have read all of the unit text selections, you will move on to a writing project. Each project will guide you through the process of writing your essay. Student models will provide guidance and help you organize your thoughts. One unit ends with an **Extended Oral Project** which will give you an opportunity to develop your oral language and communication skills.

2 Writing Process Steps

There are four steps in the writing process: Plan, Draft, Revise, and Edit and Publish. During each step, you will form and shape your writing project, and each lesson's peer review will give you the chance to receive feedback from your peers and teacher.

3 Writing Skills

Each Skill lesson focuses on a specific strategy or technique that you will use during your writing project. Each lesson presents a process for applying the skill to your own work and gives you the opportunity to practice it to improve your writing.

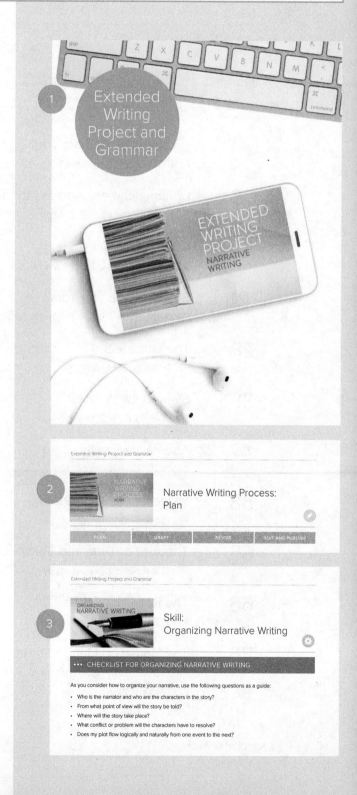

Past and Present

What makes you, you?

> Genre Focus: **POETRY**

Texts

 Paired Reading

1 I'm Nobody! Who are you?
POETRY *Emily Dickinson*

6 Commencement Address to the Santa Fe Indian School
INFORMATIONAL TEXT *Michelle Obama*

18 Curtain Call
INFORMATIONAL TEXT *Swin Cash*

21 So where are you from?
INFORMATIONAL TEXT *Naomi Sepiso*

28 The Outsiders
FICTION *S. E. Hinton*

38 Slam, Dunk, & Hook
POETRY *Yousef Komunyakaa*

47 Abuela Invents the Zero
FICTION *Judith Ortiz Cofer*

58 Inside Out & Back Again
FICTION *Thanhha Lai*

65 Theories of Time and Space
POETRY *Natasha Trethewey*

68 The Road Not Taken
POETRY *Robert Frost*

76 The House on Mango Street
FICTION *Sandra Cisneros*

Extended Writing Project and Grammar

88 | **Plan**

Organizing Argumentative Writing
Thesis Statement
Reasons and Relevant Evidence

102 | **Draft**

Introductions
Transitions
Style
Conclusions

118 | **Revise**

Grammar: Active and Passive Voice
Grammar: Verb Moods
Grammar: Consistent Verb Voice and Mood

126 | **Edit and Publish**

English Language Learner Resources

128 | **The Others**
FICTION

137 | **Mom's First Day**
FICTION

147 | Text Fulfillment through StudySync

Reading & Writing
Companion

What makes you, you?

SWIN CASH

Swin Cash (b. 1979) played fourteen seasons in the WNBA, winning three championships, appearing on four all-star teams, and winning two Olympic gold medals. In addition to her stellar playing record, she has worked to establish the WNBA players' union and to increase community involvement where she's lived. In a 2016 essay announcing her retirement, she paid tribute to the women who paved the way for her and made clear her commitment to ensuring that subsequent generations of women could play basketball professionally.

SANDRA CISNEROS

Regarded as a prominent figure in the Chicana literary movement, Sandra Cisneros (b. 1954) is a dual citizen of the United States and Mexico. In works like her classic coming-of-age novel, *The House on Mango Street* (2009), about a Latina girl growing up in a Chicago barrio, Cisneros explores themes related to Latina identity and working-class culture. In an *Electric Literature* interview, she said "the more you reach into the different things that make you who you are, the more you hold up a mirror to what makes you different from others."

JUDITH ORTIZ COFER

Born in Hormigueros, a small town in Puerto Rico, Judith Ortiz Cofer (1952–2016) moved with her family to Augusta, Georgia, at the age of fifteen. With characteristic vitality, Cofer's writing addresses the experience of living in the breach between these disparate cultures. Best known for her works of creative nonfiction, Cofer also published at least four collections of poetry, several novels, and a memoir.

EMILY DICKINSON

As early as 1850, just a few years after dropping out of Mount Holyoke and moving back into her family's estate in Amherst, Massachusetts, Emily Dickinson (1830–1886) started thinking of writing her life's work. She recognized that her aims in life were different from those of her peers and began to retreat from polite society. As a result, the speakers in Dickinson's poetry are often sharply critical of society and express a desire to be liberated from its constraints.

ROBERT FROST

Though he was born in San Francisco, Robert Frost (1874–1963) wrote mostly about New England, where he moved in 1884 following his father's death. He became known for his innovative use of New England vernacular in his writing. Objects, people, or events sparked meditations on large concepts in his poems. In "The Road Not Taken," one of Frost's most iconic poems, a fork in a woodland path becomes a metaphor.

S.E. HINTON

With her influential coming-of-age novel The Outsiders (1967) S. E. Hinton (b. 1948), who was seventeen at the time of writing, in large part inaugurated the young adult fiction genre. Set in Tulsa, Oklahoma, where she was born and has lived for the majority of her life, Hinton's novel about violence, prejudice, and class conflict in 1960s America stood out for its nuanced portrayals of teenage life. Four of Hinton's novels have been adapted into film, including *The Outsiders*, which has also been translated into thirty languages.

YUSEF KOMUNYAKAA

Born in Bogalusa, Louisiana, Yusef Komunyakaa (b. 1947) considers his first exposure to poetry to be the Old Testament–inflected cadence of his grandparents' voices. Komunyakaa would assert his distinctive style combining personal narrative, jazz rhythms, and vernacular language in two poetry collections in particular: Magic Bus (1992), about growing up in the South in the 1950s, and *Neon Vernacular: New and Selected Poems* (1994), which also dealt with the culture of the South as well as war in Southeast Asia, urban life, and music.

MICHELLE OBAMA

Lawyer, writer, public servant, and former First Lady, Michelle Obama (b. 1964) grew up on the South Side of Chicago, studied sociology and African American studies at Princeton University, and graduated from Harvard Law School. She has led initiatives to empower youth through higher education and to aid underserved communities throughout the United States, among many others. In her 2016 commencement address delivered at the Santa Fe Indian School, she reflects on how her family background shaped her character and contributed to her lifetime achievements.

NATASHA TRETHEWEY

Being born black and biracial in Gulfport, Mississippi, is one of the two "existential wounds" poet Natasha Trethewey (b. 1966) says she's been writing with her whole adult life. The other was losing her mother at the age of nineteen. In poetry collections like *Native Guard* (2006), *Bellocq's Ophelia* (2002), and *Domestic Work* (2000), she explores how her personal history is tied to larger historical narratives and the way private recollection often diverges from collective memory.

THANHHÀ LAI

Children's book author Thanhhà Lai (b. 1965) was born in Saigon, Vietnam, and immigrated to Montgomery, Alabama, in 1975. Like the main character, Hà, of her first novel, Inside Out and Back Again (2011), Lai witnessed the harsh realities of the Vietnam War, had a father who was missing in action, and fled with her family to the United States. The emotions Lai conveys through her character Hà powerfully resonate with immigrant experiences everywhere. Lai's second novel, Listen, Slowly (2015) also explores themes related to heritage and identity.

NAOMI SEPISO

Naomi Sepiso (b. 1998) is a writer of Kenyan and Zambian descent living in Australia. Her work often deals with the immigrant experience and the experience of being a young person of color. Her 2016 essay "So where are you from?" considers the sometimes damaging implications of this seemingly innocuous question.

I'm Nobody! Who are you?

POETRY
Emily Dickinson
1891

Introduction

Emily Dickinson (1830–1886), who barely left her family's house and never married, published only a handful of poems during her lifetime. After her death, hundreds more were found stacked under her bed. Today they are considered to be among the best and most influential poems ever written. In this poem, "I'm Nobody! Who are you?" Dickinson explains in a few short phrases the difference between an identity lived privately and one lived true to oneself—and the circus of life in the public eye.

"I'm Nobody! Who are you?
Are you – Nobody – too?"

1 I'm Nobody! Who are you?
2 Are you – Nobody – too?
3 Then there's a pair of us!
4 Don't tell! they'd **advertise** – you know!

5 How **dreary** – to be – Somebody!
6 How **public** – like a Frog –
7 To tell one's name – the **livelong** June –
8 To an admiring **Bog!**

Skill:
Poetic Elements
and Structure

Lines one and two rhyme, and the fourth line almost rhymes with them. For meter, the first line has 7 syllables, the next two lines have 6, the last one 8.

This stanza has irregular rhyme and meter. It begins with a rhyme scheme and then breaks out of it.

First Read

Read "I'm Nobody! Who are you?" After you read, complete the Think Questions below.

 THINK QUESTIONS

1. To whom is the speaker speaking in the first stanza? In other words, who is "you" and who are "they"? Cite textual evidence from the selection to support your answer.

2. The speaker doesn't want to be a "Somebody." Explain why she believes that being a "Somebody" is overrated. Cite specific lines in your answer.

3. In line 6, Dickinson uses a rather unusual figure of speech, or comparison, to describe what being "public" is like. Explain this comparison in line 6 in your own words. What do you think the speaker means in this line?

4. Which context clues helped you figure out the meaning of the word **advertise** in line 4? Write your own definition of *advertise* and explain how you figured out the meaning of the word.

5. Based on context clues, can you guess the definition of the word **bog** in line 8? Write your own definition of *bog* here, identifying any clues that helped you define it. Once you have written your own definition, check a print or online dictionary to verify its meaning.

Skill:
Poetic Elements and Structure

Use the Checklist to analyze Poetic Elements and Structure in "I'm Nobody! Who are you?" Refer to the sample student annotations about Poetic Elements and Structure in the text.

••• CHECKLIST FOR POETIC ELEMENTS AND STRUCTURE

In order to determine how to analyze the ways in which the structure of a text contributes to its meaning, look for the following:

- ✓ the organization of words and lines

- ✓ the relationships between words, lines, or stanzas

- ✓ the rhyme, rhythm, and meter, if present

- ✓ ways the poet uses punctuation or capitalization and how it affects the rhythm or meaning of the poem

- ✓ ways that the poem's structure connects to the poem's meaning

To analyze how poetic elements and structure contribute to a poem's meaning and style, consider the following questions:

- ✓ Do any of the words, lines, or stanzas have important similarities?

- ✓ Do any of the words, lines, or stanzas have important differences?

- ✓ Does this poem's structure relate to any of its themes?

- ✓ Does this poem's structure affect the overall meaning of the poem?

Skill:
Poetic Elements and Structure

Reread lines 5–8 of "I'm Nobody! Who are you?" Then, using the Checklist on the previous page, answer the multiple-choice questions below.

⟳ YOUR TURN

1. The word *Somebody* is capitalized in the poem because—

   ○ A. it is a proper pronoun.

   ○ B. it is the proper name of a character in the poem.

   ○ C. it conveys an idea of being well known.

   ○ D. the poet does not know how to capitalize properly.

2. The dashes mainly affect the poem by—

   ○ A. acting like periods to indicate the end of a thought.

   ○ B. breaking the flow of language so the poem is easier to read.

   ○ C. dividing the lines into sections that have the same meter.

   ○ D. emphasizing the humorous connections Dickinson makes.

Close Read

Reread "I'm Nobody! Who are you?" As you reread, complete the Skills Focus questions below. Then use your answers and annotations from the questions to help you complete the Write activity.

◎ SKILLS FOCUS

1. Compare the line structure and rhyme scheme in the first stanza (lines 1–4) to the second stanza (lines 5–8).

2. Choose a line from the poem that shows the theme. Explain how or why this line is the best choice for the theme you are discussing.

3. Choose specific words from the poem that mention characters. Also be sure to state what these characters do and how they are referenced in the poem.

4. What is something unique about this poem? Identify specific words and phrases that make this poem stand out. Also discuss what the speaker does to make her perspective different from others'.

✏ WRITE

POETRY: Write a poem in which the speaker declares who he or she is: "I'm _____." Structure your poem to include rhyme, rhythm, meter, and at least two stanzas. The poetic elements and structure should help show the speaker's attitude toward the topic and convey a theme that is important to you.

Please note that excerpts and passages in the StudySync® library and this workbook are intended as touchstones to generate interest in an author's work. The excerpts and passages do not substitute for the reading of entire texts, and StudySync® strongly recommends that students seek out and purchase the whole literary or informational work in order to experience it as the author intended. Links to online resellers are available in our digital library. In addition, complete works may be ordered through an authorized reseller by filling out and returning to StudySync® the order form enclosed in this workbook.

Reading & Writing Companion 5

Commencement Address to the Santa Fe Indian School

INFORMATIONAL TEXT
Michelle Obama
2016

Introduction

The Santa Fe Indian School is a small high school in New Mexico with a graduating class of about a hundred students. So it was much to their surprise when former First Lady Michelle Obama (b. 1964) accepted an invitation to be the school's commencement speaker. In her speech, Mrs. Obama did not shy away from acknowledging the American government's troublesome relationship with the school. The school had been founded in 1890 as an institution of enforced assimilation, during a period when the U.S. government believed the only options in dealing with Native Americans were "to civilize or exterminate them." However, the school would undergo a major transformation in the century that followed, becoming dedicated to preserving the history of its students. Today, the student body represents a multinational demographic incorporating the 22 tribal nations of New Mexico. Mrs. Obama spoke to the students about the power of education for her family and celebrated the achievements of the school's seniors, who were nearly all heading to college and had earned over five million dollars in scholarships.

"I want to tell you about the people who came before me and how they made me who I am today."

1   Please, please, be seated. Good afternoon, everyone. It is beyond an honor and a pleasure to be with you all today.

2   Of course, I want to start by thanking Hanna and Michael for their wonderful introduction. And I want to recognize all of the other outstanding student leaders who have graced us with their words today. I'm so proud of you all.

3   I also want to thank the governors, the tribal leaders, elders, the board of trustees, along with the superintendent and your amazing principal, your teachers and staff. I wish I could meet you all, I wish I could spend a whole week with you. I also want to thank the Tewa dancers who performed for us today—absolutely.

4   And of course, last but not least, to the class of 2016: You all did it! Woo! You're here! You did it! You made it! After so many long afternoons and late nights studying for exams, writing papers; after countless hours preparing to present your senior honors projects to your communities; after all those jalapeño nachos you ate at the EAC—yes, I heard about that—you did it. You're here. You made it. And we are all so very, very proud of you. I love you all so much.

5   And today, I want just to take a moment once again to look around this beautiful auditorium at the people who helped you on your journey—your families and friends, everyone in your school and your communities—all the people who pushed you and poured their love into you and believed in you even when you didn't believe in yourselves sometimes. Today is their day, too, right? So let's, graduates, give them a big, old, loud shout-out and love to our families. Thank you all. Yes!

6   And that's actually where I want to start today—with family, in particular with my own family. I want to tell you about the people who came before me and how they made me who I am today.

7   I am the great-great-granddaughter of Jim Robinson, who was born in South Carolina, lived as a slave, and is likely buried in an unmarked grave on the

Skill:
Arguments and Claims

Michelle mentions students' families and friends and the support they offered. Then she makes a statement about how her own family supported her. This claim is part of her argument: how families and friends help us on our journey.

plantation where he worked. I am the great-granddaughter of Fraser Robinson, an illiterate houseboy who taught himself to read and became an **entrepreneur,** selling newspapers and shoes. I am the granddaughter of Fraser Robinson Jr., who left the only life he'd ever known to move his family north, seeking a place where his children's dreams wouldn't be so limited by the color of their skin.

8   And I am the daughter of Fraser Robinson III and Marian Robinson, who raised me and my brother in a tiny apartment on the South Side of Chicago, just upstairs from my elderly great aunt and uncle, who my parents cared for, and just blocks away from our extended family—a host of grandparents and aunts and uncles and cousins who were always in and out of each other's homes and lives, sharing stories and food and talking and laughing for hours.

Skill:
Arguments and
Claims

Michelle gives factual information from her own life to support her argument: how families and friends help us on our journey. She talks about her mother volunteering at school and her father saving money for her college tuition.

9   And while my parents were products of segregated schools, and neither of them had an education past high school, they knew with every bone in their bodies that they wanted their kids to go to college. That was their mission from the day we were born. So my mother volunteered at our school so that she could make sure we were taking our studies seriously. And my father worked as a pump operator at the city water plant, saving every penny for our college tuition. And when my father was diagnosed with Multiple Sclerosis—a disease that affected his muscles and made it hard for him to walk and even dress himself in the morning—I remember he hardly ever missed a day of work, no matter how sick he was, no matter how much pain he was in.

10 And let me tell you, I will never forget the look of pride on his face and on my mom's face as I walked across the stage at Princeton University, and three years later at Harvard Law School to accept my diplomas—degrees that have given me opportunities that my parents never could have dreamed of for themselves.

11 So, graduates, this is my story. And I'm sharing this with you because when I heard that—when you were first brainstorming about who to invite to your commencement and someone suggested me or my husband, some of you thought that that was an impossible dream, that it just wasn't realistic to think that people like us would ever visit a school like yours. Well, today, I want you to know that there is nowhere I would rather be than right here with all of you.

12 Because while I might have grown up across the country, and while my journey may be a bit different than yours, when I learned about all of you, it was clear to me that our stories are connected, and that your values—the values that **infuse** this school—are the very same values that my parents handed down to me.

13 See, I learned respect from how my parents cared for my great aunt and uncle—how my mother would wake up in the middle of the night to check on my great aunt, how my father would prop himself up against the bathroom sink each morning, leaning hard on his crutches, to give my great uncle a shave. I learned **integrity** from my parents—that living a good life is not about being wealthy or powerful, it's about being honest and doing what you say you're going to do. It's about how you act when no one is watching, and whether you're the same person on the outside as you are on the inside.

14 My parents—yes. My parents also taught me about giving back—that when someone is sick, you show up, maybe with a home-cooked meal; when someone's down on their luck, you quietly slip them whatever's in your wallet, even if you're not doing so well yourself.

15 And finally, my parents—especially my dad—taught me about **perseverance.** See, my dad had been an athlete his whole life, a swimmer and a boxer. But if he was frustrated or disappointed by his illness, he never let on. He just woke up extra early each day, slowly fastened each button on his uniform, and eased himself down the steps one leg at a time, to get to his job and provide for our family.

16 So, graduates, I wanted to be here with you at your commencement because your values are my values—the values that carried me all the way from the South Side of Chicago to where I am today, standing before you as the First Lady of the United States. I also wanted to be here because your stories—your achievements, your contributions and the story of this school—inspire me.

17 As we all know, this school was founded as part of a **deliberate,** systematic effort to extinguish your culture; to literally annihilate who you were and what you believed in. But look at you today. The Native languages that were once strictly forbidden here now echo through hallways and in your dorm room conversations at night. The traditions that this school was

Buffalo Round Up mural at the Santa Fe Indian School

designed to destroy are now expressed in every square foot of this building— in the art on your walls, in the statue in your MSC building, in the Po Pay Day song and dance performances in your plaza, in the prayers and blessings that you offer in your heart room.

18 And the endless military drills and manual labor that those early students endured have been replaced by one of the best academic curriculums in the

country. And over the years, you all have proudly represented this school in chess tournaments, and science and robotics competitions, and every kind of internship and leadership conference imaginable. And nearly all of you are going on to college. And as the superintendent said, you've earned more than $5 million in scholarships this year. That is breathtaking—breathtaking.

19   And whether you're saying an ancient blessing over your hydroponically-grown crops, or using cutting-edge computer technology to understand the biology and hydrology of your ancestral lands, every day at this school, you've been weaving together thousands of years of your heritage with the realities of your modern lives. And all of that preparation and hard work, graduates, is so critically important, because make no mistake about it, you all are the next generation of leaders in your communities, and not years from now or decades from now, but right now.

20   Through your senior honors projects, you've already become experts on urgent issues like addiction and poverty, education and economic development. And so many of you have already stepped up to **implement** your projects in your communities, hosting a fun run to raise awareness about domestic violence and diabetes, leading a traditional foods cooking demonstration, supporting seniors and teen parents, and doing so much more.

21   And as you begin the next phase of your journey, please remember that your communities need even more of your energy and expertise. They need you to bring home additional knowledge and skills to more effectively address the challenges your communities face. That's why it is so important for all of you to hold fast to your goals, and to push through any obstacles that may come your way.

22   And here's the thing: I guarantee you that there will be obstacles—plenty of them. For example, when you get to college or wherever else you're going next, it's going to be an adjustment. College was certainly a huge adjustment for me. I had never lived away from home, away from my family for any length of time. So there were times when I felt lonely and overwhelmed during my freshman year.

23   And what I want you to remember is if that happens to you, I want you to keep pushing forward. Just keep pushing forward. And I want you to reach out and ask for help. I know your teachers tell you that all the time, but please understand that no one gets through college—or life, for that matter—alone. No one. I certainly didn't.

24   So the minute you feel like you're struggling—*the minute*—I want you to ask for help. Don't wait. Seek out a professor you trust. Go to the writing center or

the counseling center. Talk to older students who know the ropes and can give you some advice. And if the first person you ask isn't friendly or helpful, then ask a second person, and then a third and a fourth. My point is, keep asking until you get the answers you need to get you back on track. Do you understand me?

25   I am so passionate about this because your communities need you. They need you to develop your potential and become who you're meant to be. And that goes for every student in here who is thinking about dropping out, who is feeling discouraged. Your community needs you. And more than ever before, our world needs you, too.

26   And you don't need your First Lady to tell you that. All you have to do is tune in to the news and you'll see that right now, some of the loudest voices in our national conversation are saying things that go against every single one of the values that you've been living at this school. They're telling us that we should disrespect others because of who they are or where they come from or how they worship. They're telling us that we should be selfish—that folks who are struggling don't deserve our help, that we should just take what we can from life and not worry about anyone else. And they're saying that it's okay to keep harming our planet and using our land, our air, our water however we wish.

27   But, graduates, you all know that those are not the values that shape good citizens. Those are not the values that build strong families and communities and nations. You know this. So we desperately need your voices and your values in this conversation reminding us that we're all connected, we're all obligated to treat one another with respect, to act with integrity, to give back to those in need.

28   Now, I know that perhaps I'm asking a lot of all of you. And I know that sometimes all those obligations might feel like a heavy burden. I also know that many of you have already faced and overcome challenges in your lives that most young people can't even begin to imagine—challenges that have tested your courage, your confidence, your faith, and your trust.

29   But, graduates, those struggles should never be a source of shame—never— and they are certainly not a sign of weakness. Just the opposite. Those struggles are the source of your greatest strengths. Because by facing adversity head on and getting through it, you have gained wisdom and maturity beyond your years. I've seen it in you. You've developed resilience that will sustain you throughout your lives. You've deepened a well of compassion within yourselves that will help you connect with and give back to others who struggle.

Please note that excerpts and passages in the StudySync® library and this workbook are intended as touchstones to generate interest in an author's work. The excerpts and passages do not substitute for the reading of entire texts, and StudySync® strongly recommends that students seek out and purchase the whole literary or informational work in order to experience it as the author intended. Links to online resellers are available in our digital library. In addition, complete works may be ordered through an authorized reseller by filling out and returning to StudySync® the order form enclosed in this workbook.

Reading & Writing Companion   11

30   And most of all, you have taken your place in the long line of those before you whose continued survival in the face of overwhelming threats should inspire you every day of your lives—every day. I'm talking about many of your ancestors who came together to lead a revolt, risking their lives to preserve their traditions. I'm talking about your predecessors at this school who defied the rules by speaking their languages and running away to attend ceremonial dances back home. And I'm talking about the leaders who reclaimed and reopened this school for you, rebuilding it in your image and the image of your communities.

31   Graduates, all of these people, and so many more, have worked so hard and sacrificed so much so that you could be sitting in these seats on this glorious day celebrating your graduation. And as we honor their legacy today, I'm reminded of how some of your communities have seeds that your ancestors have been planting and harvesting for thousands of years, long before America was even an idea.

32   And just as they have been blessing those crops and lovingly preserving those seeds through storms and droughts, struggles and upheavals so that they could keep handing them down, generation after generation, so, too, have they handed down their wisdom, and their values and their dreams, fighting to save them in the face of unthinkable odds, spurred on by their devotion to those who came before them and those who would come after.

33   And, graduates, today, all of that—all of that—lives inside of you. All of that history, all of that sacrifice, all of that love lives within you. And you all should feel so proud and so blessed to have the privilege of continuing that story. Because with the education you've gotten from this amazing school and with the values that you've learned from your families and your communities, your big, impossible dreams are actually just the right size—big. And you have everything you need to achieve them.

34   Now, of course, it won't be easy. But standing here today with all of you, I am filled with hope. It's the same hope I feel when I think about my own story — how my great-great grandfather was another man's property, my great-grandfather was another man's servant, my grandparents and parents felt the sting of segregation and discrimination. But because they refused to be defined by anyone else's idea of who they were and what they could be, because they held fast to their impossible dreams for themselves and their children, today, my two daughters wake up each morning in the White House.

35   And every day, I try my best to pass down to my girls that same love and that same dreaming spirit that Marian and Fraser Robinson passed down to me, that same love and spirit that your ancestors passed down to all of you and that you will soon pass on to your children and grandchildren.

36   Because in the end, I believe that that is the true path of history in this country. It is long—it is. It is long. It is winding. And at times it can be very painful. But ultimately, it flows in the direction of hope, dignity and justice, because people like you stand up for your values—people like you who stay true to who you are and where you've come from, and who work every day to share the blessings you've had with others.

37   So, graduates, in closing, I hope that you will always remember your story, and that you will carry your story with you as proudly as I carry mine. I am so proud of you. I am so excited for you to continue this extraordinary journey. And I can't wait to see everything you'll achieve and bring back to your communities.

38   Thank you all. Love you.

First Read

Read "Commencement Address to the Santa Fe Indian School." After you read, complete the Think Questions below.

 THINK QUESTIONS

1. What was the Santa Fe Indian School like in its early years? What is it like when Michelle Obama speaks there in 2016? Use details from Obama's speech as evidence.

2. What advice does Michelle Obama give to students who may face difficulties in college? Cite specific evidence from the text to support your response.

3. What lessons does Michelle Obama think that the students in her audience can gain from her father's life experience? Explain, citing details from the text.

4. Use context clues to determine the meaning of **perseverance** as it is used in paragraph 15. Write your definition here and identify clues that helped you figure out its meaning.

5. Read the following dictionary entry:

   integrity
   in•teg•ri•ty \in ˈte grə dē\ *noun*

   1. the quality of having strong values or morals
   2. the state of being whole or unified
   3. the condition of being solid or sturdy in construction

   Which definition most closely matches the meaning of **integrity** as it is used in paragraph 13? Write the correct definition of *integrity* here and explain how you figured out the correct meaning.

Skill:
Arguments and Claims

Use the Checklist to analyze Arguments and Claims in "Commencement Address to the Santa Fe Indian School." Refer to the sample student annotations about Arguments and Claims in the text.

••• CHECKLIST FOR ARGUMENTS AND CLAIMS

In order to identify the speaker's argument and claims, note the following:

✓ clues that reveal the author's opinion in the title, opening remarks, or concluding statement

✓ declarative statements that come before or follow a speaker's anecdote or story

To delineate a speaker's argument and specific claims, do the following:

✓ note the information that the speaker introduces in sequential order

✓ describe the speaker's argument in your own words

To evaluate the argument and specific claims, consider the following questions:

✓ Does the writer support each claim with reasoning and evidence?

✓ Do the writer's claims work together to support the writer's overall argument?

✓ Which claims are not supported, if any?

Please note that excerpts and passages in the StudySync® library and this workbook are intended as touchstones to generate interest in an author's work. The excerpts and passages do not substitute for the reading of entire texts, and StudySync® strongly recommends that students seek out and purchase the whole literary or informational work in order to experience it as the author intended. Links to online resellers are available in our digital library. In addition, complete works may be ordered through an authorized reseller by filling out and returning to StudySync® the order form enclosed in this workbook.

Reading & Writing
Companion

15

Skill:
Arguments and Claims

Reread paragraphs 25–29 of "Commencement Address to the Santa Fe Indian School." Then, using the Checklist on the previous page, answer the multiple-choice questions below.

⟳ YOUR TURN

1. This question has two parts. First, answer Part A. Then, answer Part B.

   Part A: Which of the following statements is one claim that the speaker makes in this passage?

   ○ A. The students have already faced more difficult challenges than many other young people.

   ○ B. Many leaders are saying that it is not a problem if one causes damage to the environment.

   ○ C. The students need to use their education to contribute to their community instead of focusing on developing themselves.

   ○ D. Students can find significant strengths in the struggles that they have already overcome.

   Part B: Which of the following statements supports the claim selected in Part A?

   ○ A. "Your community needs you. And more than ever before, our world needs you, too."

   ○ B. "Because by facing adversity head on and getting through it, you have gained wisdom and maturity beyond your years. I've seen it in you."

   ○ C. "So we desperately need your voices and your values in this conversation reminding us that we're all connected, we're all obligated to treat one another with respect, to act with integrity, to give back to those in need."

   ○ D. "Now, I know that perhaps I'm asking a lot of all of you."

Close Read

Reread "Commencement Address to the Santa Fe Indian School." As you reread, complete the Skills Focus questions below. Then use your answers and annotations from the questions to help you complete the Write activity.

◎ SKILLS FOCUS

1. Identify evidence that reveals Obama's purpose for writing this speech. Explain what her purpose is and how you know.

2. What lessons does Michelle Obama think that the students in her audience can gain from her father's life? Explain her claims, citing details from the text to support your analysis.

3. Michelle Obama makes an analogy between her personal history and the history of the students at the school. Identify examples in the text where Obama describes her family's history. Using those details, explain how she might answer the question, *What makes you, you?*

✎ WRITE

ARGUMENTATIVE: Write a speech of 300 words or more to be given to students at your grade level at the end of the year. Use the First Lady's speech as a template to help you focus on a major part of your life and its history thus far: your education, your family life, your greatest achievements, or a particular struggle you've faced. Use details from that experience to write a speech that attempts to inspire graduates who are about to embark on new journeys and overcome obstacles that may have proven problematic without such advice.

Please note that excerpts and passages in the StudySync® library and this workbook are intended as touchstones to generate interest in an author's work. The excerpts and passages do not substitute for the reading of entire texts, and StudySync® strongly recommends that students seek out and purchase the whole literary or informational work in order to experience it as the author intended. Links to online resellers are available in our digital library. In addition, complete works may be ordered through an authorized reseller by filling out and returning to StudySync® the order form enclosed in this workbook.

Reading & Writing Companion   **17**

Curtain Call

INFORMATIONAL TEXT
Swin Cash
2016

Introduction

Swin Cash (b. 1979) played 14 seasons in the WNBA, winning three championships, appearing on four all-star teams, and winning two Olympic gold medals along the way. Despite all of those accomplishments, Cash was equally known for her work establishing the WNBA players' union and her involvement in the community within the various cities she played in. In 2016, she announced her upcoming retirement in this essay for *The Players' Tribune*, looking back on her proudest accomplishments and wondering what would come next.

"I've always been training for something. What happens when that's gone?"

1 While my playing career will soon be coming to an end, I will never be able to completely walk away. I care so much about whether the league will be around for another 20 years—and more. We had to fight to get where we are. We had to fight **apathy.**

2 We still fight apathy, but with trust that change will come.

3 We—the players—had to fight for the **union,** and fight to make it better. This is **critical** to our success. Many don't understand but *those are things we don't get paid for.*

4 I've done all of this because many women before me sacrificed so that I could get my shot. And I did. So why wouldn't I make sure that the **generation** behind me got theirs?

5 I remember coming into the league and seeing some of the players who helped launch the WNBA—players like Lisa Leslie, Sheryl Swoopes, Teresa Weatherspoon. They were playing not just for the love of the game, but because it was so important for the future. Futures that weren't even theirs.

6 *My* future.

7 I was part of the generation of players right after that **inaugural** wave, and we never forgot their legacy. I'm so proud now when I see my nieces dribble a basketball. That's something the women before me inspired. That's something I inspired. I would live this particular life all over again to ensure young women recognize and embrace the queens they are within.

8 This wasn't an easy decision.

9 It never is, no matter how well you've prepared.

10 Most people don't get to wake up every day and do something they're passionate about. You always feel you can give more, but at some point you have to do what's right for yourself. Maybe every athlete goes through that when they retire. It's hard to open up your hands and let go of what you know.

You hold on because it's so much a part of your routine—and your life. I've always been training for something. What happens when that's gone? I've told that kind of story about other athletes in my broadcast work, but now I'm on the other side.

11   *This is real.*

12   At the end of your career, you do a lot of **reflecting.** I've played for multiple teams in the WNBA, and they've all felt like home: Detroit and Seattle, where I won championships, and Chicago, Atlanta and New York, my last stops. And the fans in each of those cities became something like family to me. They're the reason I'm announcing my decision now. I want to spend this season showing my gratitude to everyone who's been a part of this journey. It's been rich not just because of the accomplishments and wins, but also because of the people in my life: family, teammates, mentors and fans.

13   I came into this game unapologetically fearless, as the woman I felt I was called to be. From the way I carried myself on and off the court, to using my voice for the union, to speaking out against discrimination, to fighting for all the kids in my Cash for Kids charity—all of this is bigger than me. It's bigger than my career.

14   There's no greater legacy than a legacy of lasting impact.

15   Basketball gave me the vehicle to inspire and empower. That was my purpose.

16   I have 27 regular season games left. I'll be taking in every moment as I look to the future, whatever it may hold. I understand there's a new life waiting for me after that last whistle.

17   May God allow it to be as blessed as this one has been—and a blessing to others, as well.

By Swin Cash, 2016. Reproduced by permission of The Players' Tribune.

✏ WRITE

PERSONAL RESPONSE: Swin Cash says, "Basketball gave me the vehicle to inspire and empower." Who do you want to inspire and empower? Like Swin Cash, do you have a passion that allows you to inspire others or empower those who feel powerless? What is it? Reflect on your own thoughts, feelings, or dreams for the future as you respond to each of these questions.

So where are you from?

INFORMATIONAL TEXT
Naomi Sepiso
2016

Introduction

Most people might chalk up the question "Where are you from?" as innocent small-talk. But 17-year-old Naomi Sepiso senses that for people whose appearance causes them to feel like an outsider, the question's meaning can cut much deeper. In this essay, Sepiso explains why being asked about her origin is a line in the sand between her and the asker. The question, in Sepiso's eyes, immediately ostracizes her as "the other"—someone who is from somewhere else. She describes having a "pre-rehearsed answer" she often uses, keeping her truer feelings buried beneath the many layers and complexities of her own identity.

"She was not someone from a place. She made a home of kind words and warm feelings."

NOTES

Skill:
Central or Main
Idea

I think the main idea is about belonging. "Always" shows she gets this question a lot. "Originally" sounds like someone's not Australian if they were born elsewhere. The author uses third-person like she's distancing herself from others.

1 'So where are you from?' They always asked that question; a **subtle** reminder that she was not one of them.

2 'What do you mean?' she asked. They only asked that question when they were afraid of placing her into a box. As though they were giving her the option of which box she wanted to climb into.

3 'Well... you're obviously not from here... I mean... you live here, but where are you *from*... like, originally?'

4 There it was. *Originally.* The word suggesting that she cannot **validate** her sense of belonging to this place. The **implication** being that her 'exotic' genetic makeup excludes her from her right to belong to this land.

5 She gave the long pre-rehearsed answer they often dug for. They love a good story. She told them where her mother came from, where her father came from. She told them how her parents met in a land far from their own where she was born. She told them of how they moved around from town to town and across the ocean to a place that sometimes felt like 'home'. They smiled. Happy endings always leave a crowd feeling good.

6 What she doesn't tell them is how she feels her pre-rehearsed response drag up her throat, as though she didn't pick the right words from those that whirl at the bottom of her stomach in response. She doesn't tell them that being born out of her mother's country makes her a foreigner to a land she could have called home. Or that her official documents are marked with the Coat of Arms of a land she never felt safe in. That she cannot have conversations with the grandparents she has not seen in years because her tongue will always stumble over the **nuances** of languages that never fit quite right.

7 Sometimes she felt tired of being watered down to belonging to a foreign location on a map. To being a friend that made someone else a little more 'cultured' by simple association. As though everything else she had to offer became lacking in value every time someone asked her the question.

8   She was not someone from a place. She made a home of kind words and warm feelings. Her soul became a safe nest deep inside the **confines** of her body.

"Her soul became a safe nest deep inside the confines of her body."

9   'What is the value of a land I come from. We are all of this land. We came the same way and we leave the same way.' By the time the words fought their way out of her mouth everyone else had moved on.

10 One day they would come to understand, she thought. She was not the land of her mother and father. She was her own country, with her own history of civil wars, revolutions, healing and growth. One day they would learn to keep their boxes away from her. One day they would see that she will never, *ever,* fit.

"So where are you from?" published by Sula Collective at sulacollective.com. Used by permission of Sula Collective.

Please note that excerpts and passages in the StudySync® library and this workbook are intended as touchstones to generate interest in an author's work. The excerpts and passages do not substitute for the reading of entire texts, and StudySync® strongly recommends that students seek out and purchase the whole literary or informational work in order to experience it as the author intended. Links to online resellers are available in our digital library. In addition, complete works may be ordered through an authorized reseller by filling out and returning to StudySync® the order form enclosed in this workbook.

First Read

Read "So where are you from?" After you read, complete the Think Questions below.

1. What question is the author frequently asked? Why do people use the word *originally* when they ask this question? Explain, citing evidence from the text.

2. Write two or three sentences explaining how the author's idea of where she's from differs from what other people think.

3. The author mentions a "box" in paragraph 2 and "boxes" in paragraph 10. How would you explain what she means? Cite textual evidence from the selection to support your answer.

4. Use context clues to determine the meaning of **implication** as it is used in paragraph 4 of "So where are you from?" Write your definition here and identify clues that helped you figure out its meaning.

5. Use context clues to determine the meaning of **confines** as it is used in paragraph 8. Write your definition here and identify clues that helped you figure out its meaning.

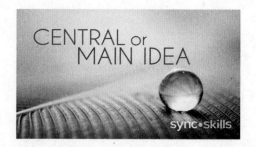

Skill:
Central or Main Idea

Use the Checklist to analyze Central or Main Idea in "So where are you from?" Refer to the sample student annotations about Central or Main Idea in the text.

••• CHECKLIST FOR CENTRAL OR MAIN IDEA

In order to identify a central or main idea of a text, note the following:

✓ the central or main idea, if it is explicitly stated

✓ when the central idea emerges

✓ ways in which supporting ideas relate to the central idea

✓ key details and supporting ideas that connect to the author's point or message

To determine a central or main idea of a text and analyze its development over the course of the text, including its relationship to supporting ideas, consider the following questions:

✓ What main idea(s) do the details in each paragraph explain or describe?

✓ What bigger idea do all the paragraphs support?

✓ What is the best way to state the central idea?

✓ How do the supporting ideas and details help develop the central idea over the course of the text?

✓ How might you objectively summarize the text and message? What details would you include?

Please note that excerpts and passages in the StudySync® library and this workbook are intended as touchstones to generate interest in an author's work. The excerpts and passages do not substitute for the reading of entire texts, and StudySync® strongly recommends that students seek out and purchase the whole literary or informational work in order to experience it as the author intended. Links to online resellers are available in our digital library. In addition, complete works may be ordered through an authorized reseller by filling out and returning to StudySync® the order form enclosed in this workbook.

Reading & Writing Companion   25

Skill:
Central or Main Idea

Reread paragraphs 7–10 of "So where are you from?" Then, using the Checklist on the previous page, answer the multiple-choice questions below.

⟳ YOUR TURN

1. This question has two parts. First, answer Part A. Then, answer Part B.

   Part A: What idea is supported by the evidence the author gives in paragraph 7?

   ○ A. The author doesn't like being valued only because she comes from a foreign place.

   ○ B. The author is flattered that others assume she is from a different country.

   ○ C. The author feels she has less value to others because she looks different.

   ○ D. The author likes people to ask where she is from so that she can tell her story.

   Part B: How does the author further develop the idea from Part A in paragraph 8?

   ○ A. She shares the story of her background with those who ask where she is from.

   ○ B. She tells readers that they should treat wherever they are living as their home.

   ○ C. She defines her version of a home as a collection of positive words and feelings that she keeps with her, not a geographic location.

   ○ D. She guesses that others must find value in positive words and feelings, and she wishes people would share those with her as well.

2. Which paragraph provides support for the author's belief that she and the others all belong to the same land?

   ○ A. 7   ○ B. 8   ○ C. 9   ○ D. 10

3. What main idea is expressed in the last paragraph?

   ○ A. The author wishes to return to the land where she fits in.

   ○ B. The author wants to be seen as her own person.

   ○ C. The author is tired of civil wars and revolutions in the world.

   ○ D. The author hopes one day that everyone will accept her.

SO WHERE ARE YOU FROM?

Close Read

Reread "So where are you from?" As you reread, complete the Skills Focus questions below. Then use your answers and annotations from the questions to help you complete the Write activity.

⊚ SKILLS FOCUS

1. Read the first and last paragraphs of "So where are you from?" and pay particular attention to the last sentence in both paragraphs. What overall idea do they share? Cite evidence from paragraphs 3–8 in support of the main or central idea.

2. How does the author's choice to use the third-person pronouns *she* and *her* support the central or main idea? Cite textual evidence.

3. It is important to the author to be accepted for the qualities that make her the individual she is. Identify examples in "So where are you from?" that show her feelings, and explain how they help make who she is.

✎ WRITE

LITERARY ANALYSIS: *Where are you from?* seems like a question with an obvious answer, but the answer is clearly more complicated according to the essay's author, Naomi Sepiso. How does Sepiso respond to this question? What supporting evidence does she include to develop her central or main idea? Be sure to use ideas and evidence from her essay to support your response.

Please note that excerpts and passages in the StudySync® library and this workbook are intended as touchstones to generate interest in an author's work. The excerpts and passages do not substitute for the reading of entire texts, and StudySync® strongly recommends that students seek out and purchase the whole literary or informational work in order to experience it as the author intended. Links to online resellers are available in our digital library. In addition, complete works may be ordered through an authorized reseller by filling out and returning to StudySync® the order form enclosed in this workbook.

Reading & Writing Companion   27

The Outsiders

FICTION
S. E. Hinton
1967

Introduction

Susan Eloise Hinton (b. 1948) was only 17 years old when her groundbreaking novel *The Outsiders* was first published. Her publisher believed the novel would sell better if the author's gender remained unknown, so it was published under Hinton's initials. The novel explores the hearts and minds of a gang with no voice, telling the story of class conflict between the lower-class "Greasers" and the upper-class "Socs" (short for "Socials" and pronounced "Soshes") in 1960's middle America. In this excerpt from early in the novel, the Greasers learn that the

"We have troubles you've never heard of. . . . Things are rough all over."

1   We were used to seeing Johnny banged up—his father clobbered him around a lot, and although it made us madder than heck, we couldn't do anything about it. But those beatings had been nothing like this. Johnny's face was cut up and bruised and swollen, and there was a wide gash from his temple to his cheekbone. He would carry that scar all his life. His white T-shirt was splattered with blood. I just stood there, trembling with sudden cold. I thought he might be dead; surely no one could be beaten like that and live. Steve closed his eyes for a second and muffled a groan as he dropped on his knees beside Soda.

2   Somehow the gang sensed what had happened. Two-Bit was suddenly there beside me, and for once his comical grin was gone and his dancing gray eyes were stormy. Darry had seen us from our porch and ran toward us, suddenly skidding to a halt. Dally was there, too, swearing under his breath, and turning away with a sick expression on his face. I wondered about it vaguely. Dally had seen people killed on the streets of New York's West Side. Why did he look sick now?

3   "Johnny?" Soda lifted him up and held him against his shoulder. He gave the limp body a slight shake. "Hey, Johnnycake."

4   Johnny didn't open his eyes, but there came a soft question. "Soda?"

5   "Yeah, it's me," Sodapop said. "Don't talk. You're gonna be okay."

6   "There was a whole bunch of them," Johnny went on, swallowing, ignoring Soda's **command.** "A blue Mustang full . . . I got so scared . . ." He tried to swear, but suddenly started crying, fighting to control himself, then sobbing all the more because he couldn't. I had seen Johnny take a whipping with a two-by-four from his old man and never let out a whimper. That made it worse to see him break now. Soda just held him and pushed Johnny's hair back out of his eyes. "It's okay, Johnnycake, they're gone now. It's okay."

7   Finally, between sobs, Johnny managed to gasp out his story. He had been hunting our football to practice a few kicks when a blue Mustang had pulled

NOTES

Skill:
Character

Ponyboy describes how Johnny often got beaten by his father, but this beating from the Socs was even worse. This helps us understand that Johnny is a character who struggles to stand up for himself. But Ponyboy and Steve both seem concerned, so we know that Johnny is also a character who has people who care about him.

Skill:
Text Evidence

These details about Johnny's story are really vivid. The text explicitly says that the Socs scared Johnny. But I can also infer that the threats from the Socs affect Johnny more than getting beaten up.

up beside the lot. There were four Socs in it. They had caught him and one of them had a lot of rings on his hand—that's what had cut Johnny up so badly. It wasn't just that they had beaten him half to death—he could take that. They had scared him. They had threatened him with everything under the sun. Johnny was high-strung anyway, a nervous wreck from getting belted every time he turned around and from hearing his parents fight all the time. Living in those conditions might have turned someone else **rebellious** and bitter; it was killing Johnny. He had never been a coward. He was a good man in a rumble. He stuck up for the gang and kept his mouth shut good around cops. But after the night of the beating, Johnny was jumpier than ever. I didn't think he'd ever get over it. Johnny never walked by himself after that. And Johnny, who was the most law-abiding of us, now carried in his back pocket a six-inch switchblade. He'd use it, too, if he ever got jumped again. They had scared him that much. He would kill the next person who jumped him. Nobody was ever going to beat him like that again. Not over his dead body. . . .

8   I had nearly forgotten that Cherry was listening to me. But when I came back to reality and looked at her, I was startled to find her as white as a sheet.

9   "All Socs aren't like that," she said. "You have to believe me, Ponyboy. Not all of us are like that."

10   "Sure," I said.

11   "That's like saying all you greasers are like Dallas Winston. I'll bet he's jumped a few people."

12   I **digested** that. It was true. Dally had jumped people. He had told us stories about muggings in New York that had made the hair on the back of my neck stand up. But not all of us are that bad.

13   Cherry no longer looked sick, only sad. "I'll bet you think the Socs have it made. The rich kids, the West-side Socs. I'll tell you something, Ponyboy, and it may come as a surprise. We have troubles you've never heard of. You want to know something?" She looked me straight in the eye. "Things are rough all over."

14   "I believe you," I said. "We'd better get out there with the popcorn or Two-Bit'll think I ran off with his money."

• • •

15   After the movie was over it suddenly came to us that Cherry and Marcia didn't have a way to get home. Two-Bit **gallantly** offered to walk them home—the west side of town was only about twenty miles away—but they wanted to call

their parents and have them come and get them. Two-Bit finally talked them into letting us drive them home in his car. I think they were still half-scared of us. They were getting over it, though, as we walked to Two-Bit's house to pick up the car. It seemed funny to me that Socs—if these girls were any example— were just like us. They liked the Beatles and thought Elvis Presley was out, and we thought the Beatles were rank and that Elvis was tuff, but that seemed the only difference to me. Of course greasy girls would have acted a lot tougher, but there was a basic sameness. I thought maybe it was money that separated us.

16 "No," Cherry said slowly when I said this. "It's not just money. Part of it is, but not all. You Greasers have a different set of values. You're more emotional. We're **sophisticated**—cool to the point of not feeling anything. Nothing is real with us. You know, sometimes I'll catch myself talking to a girl-friend, and I realize I don't mean half of what I'm saying. I don't really think a beer blast on the river bottom is super-cool, but I'll rave about one to a girl-friend just to be saying something." She smiled at me. "I never told anyone that. I think you're the first person I've ever really gotten through to."

Excerpted from *The Outsiders* by S. E. Hinton, published by the Penguin Group.

Please note that excerpts and passages in the StudySync® library and this workbook are intended as touchstones to generate interest in an author's work. The excerpts and passages do not substitute for the reading of entire texts, and StudySync® strongly recommends that students seek out and purchase the whole literary or informational work in order to experience it as the author intended. Links to online resellers are available in our digital library. In addition, complete works may be ordered through an authorized reseller by filling out and returning to StudySync® the order form enclosed in this workbook.

Reading & Writing Companion

31

First Read

Read *The Outsiders*. After you read, complete the Think Questions below.

1. How would you describe the relationships among the Greasers? Cite textual evidence from the selection to support your answer.

2. What effect does the attack have on Johnny? Cite textual evidence from the selection to support your answer.

3. What observation does Ponyboy make about the Greasers and the Socs? Cite textual evidence from the selection to support your answer.

4. Use context clues to determine the meaning of **gallantly** as it is used in paragraph 15 of the excerpt from *The Outsiders*. Write your definition here and identify clues that helped you figure out its meaning.

5. Read the following dictionary entry:

   digest
   di•gest \dī ˈjest\ *verb*

   1. to break down food into a form that the body can use
   2. to think about something and try to understand it
   3. to arrange in a particular order

   Which definition most closely matches the meaning of **digested** as it is used in paragraph 12? Write the correct definition of *digested* here and explain how you figured out the correct meaning.

Skill:
Character

Use the Checklist to analyze Character in *The Outsiders*. Refer to the sample student annotations about Character in the text.

••• CHECKLIST FOR CHARACTER

In order to determine how dialogue or incidents in a story propel the action, reveal aspects of a character, or provoke a decision, note the following:

- ✓ the characters in the story, including the protagonist and antagonist

- ✓ key dialogue and how it reveals character traits and moves the action, or the events of the plot, forward

- ✓ characters' responses and reactions to other characters or events, and what this reveals about them

- ✓ when an event or another character's actions or dialogue provokes a character to make a decision

- ✓ the resolution and ways it affects the characters

To analyze how particular lines of dialogue or incidents in a story or drama propel the action, reveal aspects of a character, or provoke a decision, consider the following questions:

- ✓ How does the dialogue propel, or move forward, the action in the story?

- ✓ How does the dialogue reveal different aspects or traits of each character?

- ✓ How do the events, actions, and reactions reveal different aspects or traits of each character?

- ✓ Did an event or a character provoke another character to make a decision? What was it, and how did it affect the events of the plot?

- ✓ How does the resolution affect the characters?

Skill: Character

Reread paragraphs 15 and 16 of *The Outsiders*. Then, using the Checklist on the previous page, answer the multiple-choice questions below.

YOUR TURN

1. Based on Two-Bit's offer to help Cherry and Marcia get home in paragraph 15, the reader can conclude that—

   ○ A. Two-Bit is a nice guy, despite the reputation that most Greasers have.
   ○ B. Two-Bit is just as bad as his Greaser reputation implies.
   ○ C. Cherry and Marcia are afraid of Two-Bit and acting out of fear.
   ○ D. Cherry and Marcia do not want to owe the Greasers any favors.

2. Based on the dialogue between Ponyboy and Cherry in paragraphs 15 and 16, the reader can conclude that both characters share which of the following character traits?

   ○ A. Both Cherry and Ponyboy are lonely for company.
   ○ B. Both Cherry and Ponyboy are tough.
   ○ C. Both Cherry and Ponyboy are becoming aware of the commonalities they share.
   ○ D. Both Cherry and Ponyboy are stubborn when it comes to seeing things from another perspective.

3. Which piece of dialogue best shows that Cherry feels pressure to fit in with the Socs?

   ○ A. "You Greasers have a different set of values."
   ○ B. "We're sophisticated—cool to the point of not feeling anything."
   ○ C. "You know, sometimes I'll catch myself talking to a girl-friend, and I realize I don't mean half of what I'm saying."
   ○ D. "I never told anyone that. I think you're the first person I've ever really gotten through to."

Skill:
Textual Evidence

Use the Checklist to analyze Textual Evidence in "The Outsiders." Refer to the sample student annotations about Textual Evidence in the text.

••• CHECKLIST FOR TEXTUAL EVIDENCE

In order to support an analysis by citing textual evidence that is explicitly stated in the text, do the following:

- ✓ read the text closely and critically

- ✓ identify what the text says explicitly

- ✓ find the most relevant textual evidence that supports your analysis

- ✓ consider why an author explicitly states specific details and information

- ✓ cite the specific words, phrases, sentences, or paragraphs from the text that support your analysis

- ✓ cite evidence from the text that most strongly supports your analysis

In order to interpret implicit meanings in a text by making inferences, do the following:

- ✓ combine information directly stated in the text with your own knowledge, experiences, and observations

- ✓ cite the specific words, phrases, sentences, or paragraphs from the text that support this inference

In order to cite textual evidence to support an analysis of what the text says explicitly as well as inferences drawn from the text, consider the following questions:

- ✓ Have I read the text closely and critically?

- ✓ What inferences am I making about the text? What textual evidence am I using to support these inferences?

- ✓ Am I quoting the evidence from the text correctly?

- ✓ Does my textual evidence logically relate to my analysis?

- ✓ What textual evidence from the text most strongly supports your analysis?

Skill:
Textual Evidence

Reread the end of paragraph 7 from "The Outsiders." Then, using the Checklist on the previous page, answer the multiple-choice questions below.

↻ YOUR TURN

1. Which of the following inferences can be supported by specific textual evidence from the passage?

   ○ A. Johnny had been the calmest one of the Greasers before the beating.
   ○ B. The beating by the Socs changed Johnny, perhaps permanently.
   ○ C. Being beaten by his father had made Johnny afraid of authority.
   ○ D. The beating by the Socs turned Johnny, who had been brave, into a coward.

2. Which sentence from the passage supports your answer to the previous question?

   ○ A. "Johnny was high-strung anyway, a nervous wreck from getting belted every time he turned around and from hearing his parents fight all the time."
   ○ B. "He stuck up for the gang and kept his mouth shut good around cops."
   ○ C. "But after that night of the beating, Johnny was jumpier than ever. I didn't think he'd ever get over it."
   ○ D. "Living in those conditions might have turned someone else rebellious and bitter; it was killing Johnny."

3. Why does the text say that Johnny "now carried in his back pocket a six-inch switchblade?"

   ○ A. It says he carried a switchblade because "he had always been a coward."
   ○ B. It says he decided "he would kill the next" Socs member he found.
   ○ C. It says that Johnny would "use it" to "kill the next person who jumped him." which shows that he might be afraid but will protect himself at all costs from now on.
   ○ D. It says his father gave it to him after the beating.

 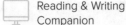

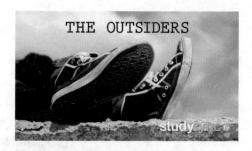

THE OUTSIDERS

study

Close Read

Reread *The Outsiders*. As you reread, complete the Skills Focus questions below. Then use your answers and annotations from the questions to help you complete the Write activity.

◎ SKILLS FOCUS

1. Identify clues in the text that reveal the character traits that the Greasers all possess. Explain how this textual evidence about the group helps you infer a theme of the excerpt.

2. Explain how the incident with the Socs changed Johnny's character.

3. Identify evidence from the text that helps you understand Cherry's unique character traits.

4. How might the Greasers and the Socs answer the question *What makes you, you?* Identify details that show what influences one group's identity, and explain how they see themselves in relation to others.

✐ WRITE

LITERARY ANALYSIS: One theme of the novel *The Outsiders* has to do with the pressure to remain loyal to a group. Explain how interacting with Cherry has changed Ponyboy's understanding of similarities and differences between the Greasers and the Socs. How does his conversation with Cherry begin to change his overall character? Be sure to support your ideas with evidence from the text.

Please note that excerpts and passages in the StudySync® library and this workbook are intended as touchstones to generate interest in an author's work. The excerpts and passages do not substitute for the reading of entire texts, and StudySync® strongly recommends that students seek out and purchase the whole literary or informational work in order to experience it as the author intended. Links to online resellers are available in our digital library. In addition, complete works may be ordered through an authorized reseller by filling out and returning to StudySync® the order form enclosed in this workbook.

Reading & Writing Companion   **37**

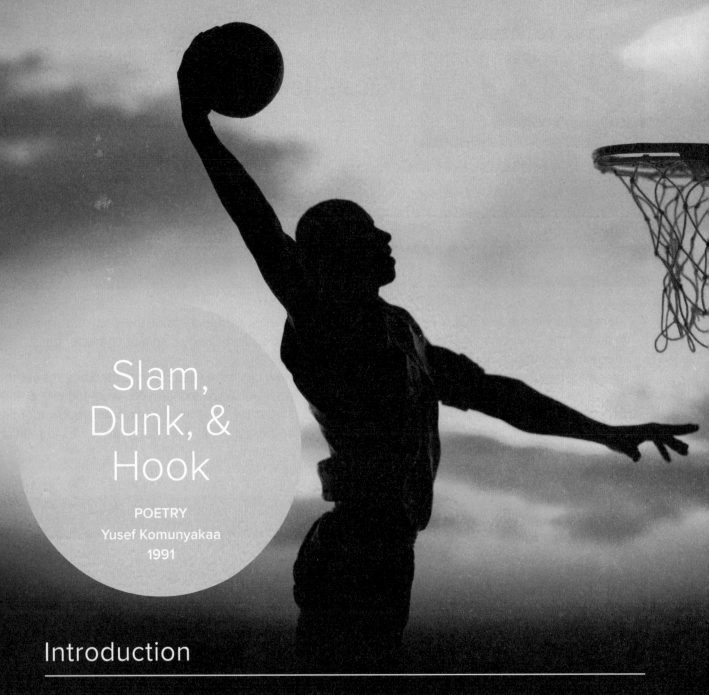

Slam, Dunk, & Hook

POETRY
Yusef Komunyakaa
1991

Introduction

"**S**lam, Dunk, & Hook" is a poem by Pulitzer Prize-winning poet Yusef Komunyakaa (b. 1947). It is included in Komunyakaa's *Magic Bus*, his 1992 collection of poems that draw on his experiences growing up as an African American in the 1950s in Bogalusa, a small city in northeastern Louisiana. While "Slam, Dunk, & Hook" primarily describes the feelings of playing basketball as a youth, the racial tensions that defined the 1950s Deep South seem to exist just outside the edges of both the poem and the "roundhouse" where the boys play

"Lay ups. Fast breaks.

1 Fast breaks. Lay ups. With Mercury's
2 **Insignia** on our sneakers,
3 We outmaneuvered to footwork
4 Of bad angels. Nothing but a hot
5 Swish of strings like silk
6 Ten feet out. In the roundhouse
7 **Labyrinth** our bodies
8 Created, we could almost
9 Last forever, **poised** in midair
10 Like storybook sea monsters.
11 A high note hung there
12 A long second. Off
13 The rim. We'd corkscrew
14 Up & dunk balls that exploded
15 The skullcap of hope & good
16 Intention. Lanky, all hands
17 & feet . . . sprung **rhythm**.
18 We were **metaphysical** when girls
19 Cheered on the sidelines.
20 Tangled up in a falling,
21 Muscles were a bright motor
22 Double-flashing to the metal hoop
23 Nailed to our oak.
24 When Sonny Boy's mama died
25 He played nonstop all day, so hard
26 Our backboard splintered.
27 Glistening with sweat,
28 We rolled the ball off
29 Our fingertips. Trouble
30 Was there slapping a blackjack
31 Against an open palm.
32 Dribble, drive to the inside,
33 & glide like a sparrow hawk.
34 Lay ups. Fast breaks.
35 We had moves we didn't know

NOTES

Skill:
Poetic Elements
and Structure

There's no regular meter or rhyme scheme, so this is open form. The line breaks and capitalized words within the lines make me pause and imagine the "sneakers" and "footwork." When I read this aloud, the rhythm sounds like a basketball pounding on the court.

Skill:
Allusion

Sea monsters are powerful creatures from folklore. I've seen movies where they rise up out of the sea to attack ships. As with the allusion to Mercury at the beginning of the poem, the speaker is describing the players as having superhuman qualities.

NOTES

36 We had. Our bodies spun
37 On swivels of bone & faith,
38 Through a lyric slipknot
39 Of joy, & we knew we were
40 Beautiful & dangerous.

"Slam, Dunk, & Hook" from *Pleasure Dome: New and Collected Poems.*

First Read

Read "Slam, Dunk, & Hook." After you read, complete the Think Questions below.

 THINK QUESTIONS

1. What do lines 1–17 of the poem describe? Who appears in these lines? Cite textual evidence from the poem to support your answer.

2. What troubling event happens to Sonny Boy? How does he react? Use textual evidence to support your answer.

3. What words and phrases suggest the power and beauty of the basketball game? Explain your answer.

4. Read lines 6–9. Then use context clues to determine the meaning of **labyrinth** as it is used in the poem.

5. Read the following dictionary entry:

   poised
   poised \ poizd \ *adjective*

   1. marked by balance or equilibrium
   2. having a composed or self-assured manner

   Explain which definition most closely matches the meaning of **poised** as it is used in line 9. Do you think either of these meanings could work, or is one more accurate than the other? Explain.

Please note that excerpts and passages in the StudySync® library and this workbook are intended as touchstones to generate interest in an author's work. The excerpts and passages do not substitute for the reading of entire texts, and StudySync® strongly recommends that students seek out and purchase the whole literary or informational work in order to experience it as the author intended. Links to online resellers are available in our digital library. In addition, complete works may be ordered through an authorized reseller by filling out and returning to StudySync® the order form enclosed in this workbook.

Reading & Writing Companion   **41**

Skill:
Poetic Elements and Structure

Use the Checklist to analyze Poetic Elements and Structure in "Slam, Dunk, & Hook." Refer to the sample student annotations about Poetic Elements and Structure in the text.

••• CHECKLIST FOR POETIC ELEMENTS AND STRUCTURE

In order to determine how to compare and contrast the structures of two or more poems, look for the following:

- ✓ the forms and overall structures of the poems

- ✓ the rhyme, rhythm, and meter, if present

- ✓ lines and stanzas in the poems that suggest the poems' meanings and styles

- ✓ ways that the poems' structures connect to the poems' meanings

To compare and contrast the structures of two or more poems and analyze how the differing structures contribute to each poem's meaning and style, consider the following questions:

- ✓ What forms do the poets use?

- ✓ How do the poems compare to each other in their structures?

- ✓ How does the choice of form or structure affect the overall meaning of each poem? How do they compare?

Skill:
Poetic Elements and Structure

Reread lines 27–40 of "Slam, Dunk, & Hook." Then, using the Checklist on the previous page, answer the multiple-choice questions below.

↻ YOUR TURN

1. The capital letter *T* in *Trouble* in line 29 shows—

   ○ A. the beginning of a new thought.

   ○ B. the beginning of a new line in the poem.

   ○ C. a proper noun.

   ○ D. a mistake because it should not be a capital letter.

2. Line 34 in the poem is an example of—

   ○ A. the use of rhyme in the poem.

   ○ B. the complete thought contained in each line.

   ○ C. the short lines in the structure of the poem.

   ○ D. the use of repetition in the poem.

3. Which lines have one complete thought that best sums up the meaning of the poem?

   ○ A. lines 27–29

   ○ B. lines 31–32

   ○ C. lines 32–33

   ○ D. lines 36–40

Skill:
Allusion

Use the Checklist to analyze Poetic Elements and Structure in "Slam, Dunk, & Hook." Refer to the sample student annotations about Poetic Elements and Structure in the text.

••• CHECKLIST FOR ALLUSION

In order to identify an allusion, note the following:

✓ references or clues that suggest a reference to a myth, mythological creature, famous person, historical event, work of art, or work of literature

✓ the theme, event, character, or situation in a text to which the references or clues add information

✓ patterns of events or character types

To better understand the allusion in a work of literature, do the following:

✓ use a print or digital resource to look up what you think might be an allusion

✓ list details about the allusion that relate to themes, events, or character types

To analyze how a modern work of fiction or poetry draws on themes, events, patterns of events, or character types from myths, traditional stories, or religious works and describe how the material is rendered new, consider the following questions:

✓ What theme/event/character is referenced in the text I am reading? How do I know?

✓ How does that theme/event/character relate to what is happening in this new text?

✓ What does the modern version add to the previous story?

✓ How does the inclusion of allusions impact the meaning or tone of the story or poem?

Skill:
Allusion

Reread lines 3–17 of "Slam, Dunk, & Hook." Then, using the Checklist on the previous page, answer the multiple-choice questions below.

⟳ YOUR TURN

1. Which phrase from the poem is a Biblical allusion that describes the opponents of the players as supernatural creatures who have fallen from grace?

   ○ A. "We outmaneuvered to footwork / Of bad angels."

   ○ B. "A high note hung there / A long second."

   ○ C. "We'd corkscrew / Up & dunk balls"

   ○ D. "Lanky, all hands / & feet . . . sprung rhythm."

2. Which phrase from the poem is an allusion to a Greek myth that involves a complicated system of moving around?

   ○ A. "Nothing but a hot / Swish of strings like silk"

   ○ B. "In the roundhouse / Labyrinth our bodies / Created"

   ○ C. "we could almost / Last forever, poised in midair"

   ○ D. "The skullcap of hope & good / Intention."

Close Read

Reread "Slam, Dunk, & Hook." As you reread, complete the Skills Focus questions below. Then use your answers and annotations from the questions to help you complete the Write activity.

◎ SKILLS FOCUS

1. Look at the first lines of the poem. From whose point of view is the poem being told? How does this information help to establish and contribute to the poetic structure of the poem? Cite specific textual evidence to help support your claims.

2. Identify the connection between line length and meaning in the poem. Cite evidence from lines in the poem.

3. Allusion is a brief reference to a work of art, a character from a myth or story, or an event in history. For example, a mention of Scrooge is an allusion to a character in *A Christmas Carol* by

Charles Dickens. Identify examples of allusion in "Slam, Dunk, & Hook." Explain how the allusions add to your understanding.

4. Analyze the line breaks in the poem. What types of words appear at the ends of lines? What effect do they have on the meaning of the poem?

5. Is there a sport or activity that makes you feel as passionate as Komunyakaa feels about basketball? Citing specific evidence from the text, respond to Komunyakaa's attitude towards basketball based on your experience.

✎ WRITE

DISCUSSION: How is the identity of the speaker and other basketball players tied to the game of basketball? Discuss this question with a group of your peers. To prepare for your discussion, use the graphic organizer to identify the poet's use of structure and allusions, and explain how they help communicate the game's importance to the identity of individual players and the team as a whole. After your discussion, you will write a reflection.

Abuela Invents the Zero

FICTION
Judith Ortiz Cofer
1996

Introduction

The writings of Judith Ortiz Cofer (1952–2016) writing reflects the differences between her two childhood homes: one on the island of Puerto Rico and one in a barrio (neighborhood) on the mainland. In this short story, Constancia is a teenager whose abuela (grandmother) comes to visit her in New Jersey. Caught between her American and Puerto Rican identities, Constancia feels embarrassed by the "bizarre" behavior of her abuela at church and hides her face in shame. Later,

"You made me feel like a zero, like a nothing."

1 "You made me feel like a zero, like a nothing," she says in Spanish, *un cero, nada*. She is trembling, an angry little old woman lost in a heavy winter coat that belongs to my mother. And I end up being sent to my room, like I was a child, to think about my grandmother's idea of math.

2 It all began with Abuela coming up from the Island for a visit—her first time in the United States. My mother and father paid her way here so that she wouldn't die without seeing snow, though if you asked me, and nobody has, the dirty slush in this city is not worth the price of a ticket. But I guess she deserves some kind of award for having had ten kids and survived to tell about it. My mother is the youngest of the bunch. Right up to the time when we're supposed to pick up the old lady at the airport, my mother is telling me stories about how hard times were for *la familia* on *la isla,* and how *la abuela* worked night and day to support them after their father died of a heart attack. I'd die of a heart attack too if I had a troop like that to support. Anyway, I had seen her only three or four times in my entire life, whenever we would go for somebody's funeral. I was born here and I have lived in this building all my life. But when Mami says, "Connie, please be nice to Abuela. She doesn't have too many years left. Do you promise me, Constancia?"—when she uses my full name, I know she means business. So I say, "Sure." Why wouldn't I be nice? I'm not a monster, after all.

**Skill:
Plot**

It seems strange that Connie would have to promise to be nice to her own grandmother. I wonder if this dialogue hints at a source of conflict in the story between Connie and her parents.

3 So we go to Kennedy to get *la abuela,* and she is the last to come out of the airplane, on the arm of the cabin attendant, all wrapped up in a black shawl. He hands her over to my parents like she was a package sent airmail. It is January, two feet of snow on the ground, and she's wearing a shawl over a thick black dress. That's just the start.

4 Once home, she refuses to let my mother buy her a coat because it's a waste of money for the two weeks she'll be in *el Polo Norte,* as she calls New Jersey, the North Pole. So since she's only four feet eleven inches tall, she walks around in my mother's big black coat looking ridiculous. I try to walk far behind them in public so that no one will think we're together. I plan to stay very busy the whole time she's with us so that I won't be asked to take her anywhere, but my plan is ruined when my mother comes down with the flu

and Abuela absolutely *has* to attend Sunday mass or her soul will be eternally damned. She's more Catholic than the Pope. My father decides that he should stay home with my mother and that I should escort *la abuela* to church. He tells me this on Saturday night as I'm getting ready to go out to the mall with my friends.

5   "No way," I say.

6   I go for the car keys on the kitchen table: he usually leaves them there for me on Friday and Saturday nights. He beats me to them.

7   "No way," he says, pocketing them and grinning at me.

8   Needless to say, we come to a **compromise** very quickly. I do have a responsibility to Sandra and Anita, who don't drive yet. There is a Harley-Davidson fashion show at Brookline Square that we *cannot* miss.

9   "The mass in Spanish is at ten sharp tomorrow morning, *entiendes*?" My father is dangling the car keys in front of my nose and pulling them back when I try to reach for them. He's really enjoying himself.

10 "I understand. Ten o'clock. I'm out of here." I pry his fingers off the key ring. He knows that I'm late, so he makes it just a little difficult. Then he laughs. I run out of our apartment before he changes his mind. I have no idea what I'm getting myself into.

11 Sunday morning I have to walk two blocks on dirty snow to retrieve the car. I warm it up for Abuela as instructed by my parents, and drive it to the front of our building. My father walks her by the hand in baby steps on the slippery snow. The sight of her little head with a bun on top of it sticking out of that huge coat makes me want to run back into my room and get under the covers. I just hope that nobody I know sees us together. I'm dreaming, of course. The mass is packed with people from our block. It's a holy day of **obligation** and everyone I ever met is there.

12 I have to help her climb the steps, and she stops to take a deep breath after each one, then I lead her down the aisle so that everybody can see me with my bizarre grandmother. If I were a good Catholic, I'm sure I'd get some purgatory time taken off for my sacrifice. She is walking as slow as Captain Cousteau exploring the bottom of the sea, looking around, taking her sweet time. Finally she chooses a pew, but she wants to sit in the other end. It's like she had a spot picked out for some unknown reason, and although it's the most inconvenient seat in the house, that's where she has to sit. So we squeeze by all the people already sitting there, saying, "Excuse me, please, *con permiso*, pardon me," getting annoyed looks the whole way. By the time

Skill:
Plot

Connie already regrets taking Abuela to mass. She is embarrassed to be seen with her grandmother and more concerned about what others will think. I think Connie's feelings will lead to the central conflict with Abuela.

NOTES

we settle in, I'm drenched in sweat. I keep my head down like I'm praying so as not to see or be seen. She is praying loud, in Spanish, and singing hymns at the top of her creaky voice.

13   I ignore her when she gets up with a hundred other people to go take communion. I'm actually praying hard now—that this will all be over soon. But the next time I look up, I see a black coat dragging around and around the church, stopping here and there so a little gray head can peek out like a **periscope** on a submarine. There are giggles in the church, and even the priest has frozen in the middle of a blessing, his hands above his head like he is about to lead the congregation in a set of jumping jacks.

Skill:
Theme

Abuela gets lost in church, forcing Connie, the narrator, to make a choice. This choice is uncomfortable for Connie, so she decides to stay seated. It's clear she doesn't want to be seen in public with her grandmother.

14   I realize to my horror that my grandmother is lost. She can't find her way back to the pew. I am so embarrassed that even though the woman next to me is shooting daggers at me with her eyes, I just can't move to go get her. I put my hands over my face like I'm praying, but it's really to hide my burning cheeks. I would like for her to disappear. I just know that on Monday my friends, and my enemies, in the barrio will have a lot of **senile**-grandmother jokes to tell in front of me. I am frozen to my seat. So the same woman who wants me dead on the spot does it for me. She makes a big deal out of getting up and hurrying to get Abuela.

15   The rest of the mass is a blur. All I know is that my grandmother kneels the whole time with her hands over *her* face. She doesn't speak to me on the way home, and she doesn't let me help her walk, even though she almost falls a couple of times.

16   When we get to the apartment, my parents are at the kitchen table, where my mother is trying to eat some soup. They can see right away that something is wrong. Then Abuela points her finger at me like a judge passing a **sentence** on a criminal. She says in Spanish, "You made me feel like a zero, like a nothing." Then she goes to her room.

17   I try to explain what happened. "I don't understand why she's so upset. She just got lost and wandered around for a while," I tell them. But it sounds lame, even to my own ears. My mother gives me a look that makes me cringe and goes in to Abuela's room to get her version of the story. She comes out with tears in her eyes.

18   "Your grandmother says to tell you that of all the hurtful things you can do to a person, the worst is to make them feel as if they are worth nothing."

19   I can feel myself shrinking right there in front of her. But I can't bring myself to tell my mother that I think I understand how I made Abuela feel. I might be sent into the old lady's room to apologize, and it's not easy to admit you've

been a jerk—at least, not right away with everybody watching. So I just sit there not saying anything.

20 My mother looks at me for a long time, like she feels sorry for me. Then she says, "You should know, Constancia, that if it wasn't for the old woman whose existence you don't seem to value, you and I would not be here."

21 That's when *I'm* sent to *my* room to consider a number I hadn't thought much about—until today.

"Abuela Invents the Zero" from *An Island Like You: Stories of the Barrio* by Judith Ortiz Cofer and published by Scholastic, Inc. Copyright (c) 1995 by Judith Ortiz Cofer. Reprinted with permission. All rights reserved.

First Read

Read "Abuela Invents the Zero." After you read, complete the Think Questions below.

 THINK QUESTIONS

1. Describe Constancia's relationship with Abuela prior to her grandmother's visit to New Jersey. Cite details from the text to support your response.

2. Refer to details from the text to explain why Constancia considers her grandmother to be, in her eyes, "ridiculous" and "bizarre."

3. How does Constancia respond when Abuela becomes lost in the church? Describe her reaction, and support your answer with evidence from the text.

4. Use context to determine the meaning of the word **obligation** as it is used in "Abuela Invents the Zero" in paragraph 11. Write your definition of *obligation* here and explain how you found it.

5. Read the following dictionary entry:

sentence
sen•tence \ˈsen(t)əns \

noun

1. a complete statement, command, question, etc., containing one or more words
2. a punishment given for a particular offense

verb

1. to punish or pass judgment (on someone), typically in a court of law

Which definition most closely matches the meaning of **sentence** as it is used in paragraph 16? Write the appropriate definition of *sentence* here and explain how you figured out the correct meaning.

PLOT

Skill:
Plot

Use the Checklist to analyze Plot in "Abuela Invents the Zero." Refer to the sample student annotations about Plot in the text.

••• CHECKLIST FOR PLOT

In order to identify plot elements in a story or drama, note the following:

- ✓ dialogue or conversations between two or more characters

- ✓ incidents or notable events throughout the story's plot

- ✓ central conflict

- ✓ characters' responses to or decisions about incidents

- ✓ the ways in which the characters affect the resolution of the conflict

To analyze how particular lines of dialogue or incidents in a story or drama propel the action or provoke a decision, consider the following questions:

- ✓ What happens as a result of a dialogue between two characters?

- ✓ How does the plot unfold in the story?

- ✓ Do characters respond or change as the plot advances? How?

- ✓ What causes a character to act or make a decision? What events occur as a result of these actions or decisions?

Please note that excerpts and passages in the StudySync® library and this workbook are intended as touchstones to generate interest in an author's work. The excerpts and passages do not substitute for the reading of entire texts, and StudySync® strongly recommends that students seek out and purchase the whole literary or informational work in order to experience it as the author intended. Links to online resellers are available in our digital library. In addition, complete works may be ordered through an authorized reseller by filling out and returning to StudySync® the order form enclosed in this workbook.

Reading & Writing Companion   53

PLOT

Skill:
Plot

Reread paragraphs 4–10 of "Abuela Invents the Zero." Then, using the Checklist on the previous page, answer the multiple-choice questions below.

⟳ YOUR TURN

1. How does the decision that Connie's father makes in paragraph 4 affect the events that follow?

   ○ A. Connie's father decides that Connie should take Abuela to church.

   ○ B. Connie's mother comes down with the flu.

   ○ C. Connie's father tells her that she should take Abuela to church and Connie refuses.

   ○ D. Abuela decides she doesn't need to go to church.

2. How does the dialogue in paragraphs 5–7 influence the decision Connie makes about taking Abuela to church?

   ○ A. The dialogue in paragraphs 5–7 influences Connie to take Abuela to the Brookline Square Mall.

   ○ B. Connie decides to take Abuela to church because her father says "No way" when she asks for the car keys to head to a fashion show.

   ○ C. Connie decides to take Abuela to church because her father says she has to.

   ○ D. Connie tells her father "No way" when he tells her to take Abuela to church because she wants to go to the fashion show.

Skill: Theme

Use the Checklist to analyze Theme in "Abuela Invents the Zero." Refer to the sample student annotations about Theme in the text.

••• YOUR TURN

In order to identify a theme or central idea of a text, note the following:

✓ the subject of the text and a theme that might be stated directly in the text

✓ details in the text that help to reveal theme

- the title and chapter headings
- details about the setting
- a narrator's or speaker's tone
- characters' thoughts, actions, and dialogue
- the central conflict in a story's plot
- the climax, or turning point, in the story
- the resolution of the conflict
- shifts in characters, setting, or plot events

✓ analyze the development of the theme and its relationship to the characters, setting, and plot

- the time and place, such as a narrative set in the past or future, can affect how a character responds to events
- characters' responses and reactions to events in a text can reveal themes in a story
- the story's conflict or resolution may help to determine the theme

To determine a theme or central idea of a text and analyze its development over the course of the text, including its relationship to the characters, setting, and plot, use the following questions as a guide:

✓ What is a theme or central idea of the text? When did you become aware of that theme?

✓ How does the theme relate to the characters, setting, and plot?

✓ How does the theme develop over the course of the text?

Skill:
Theme

Reread paragraphs 15–17 of "Abuela Invents the Zero." Then, using the Checklist on the previous page, answer the multiple-choice questions below.

↻ YOUR TURN

1. Referring to paragraph 15, how does Abuela react to Connie?

   ○ A. She seeks help from her granddaughter and uses her for support.
   ○ B. She apologizes to her granddaughter for embarrassing her in church.
   ○ C. She ignores her granddaughter and refuses Connie's help.
   ○ D. She is angry with her granddaughter and yells at her on the way home.

2. Which quote from the story demonstrates how Abuela feels about Connie's behavior in church?

   ○ A. She says in Spanish, "You made me feel like a zero, like a nothing."
   ○ B. I try to explain what happened. "I don't understand why she's so upset. She just got lost and wandered around for a while," I tell them.
   ○ C. They can see right away that something is wrong.
   ○ D. But I can't bring myself to tell my mother that I think I understand how I made Abuela feel.

3. Referring to paragraph 17, whose reaction changes the narrator's opinion of her grandmother?

   ○ A. Her parents' reaction when they can see right away that something is wrong.
   ○ B. Abuela's reaction when she says in Spanish, "You made me feel like a zero, like a nothing."
   ○ C. Abuela's reaction when she doesn't speak on the way home.
   ○ D. Her mother's reaction when she has tears in her eyes and tells her what Abuela said.

Close Read

Reread "Abuela Invents the Zero." As you reread, complete the Skills Focus questions below. Then use your answers and annotations from the questions to help you complete the Write activity.

◎ SKILLS FOCUS

1. Which lines of dialogue in the story reveal that Connie is unaware of the consequences her actions can have? Cite evidence in the text to support your answer.

2. Analyzing specific incidents and events in a story or drama can help readers determine the theme as it develops over the course of the text. Reread paragraphs 13–15. Cite specific evidence that suggests the incident at the church is a turning point in the relationship between Connie and Abuela, and what it reveals or communicates about the theme.

3. How does the author reveal the importance Connie places on clothes and appearance throughout the story, and how does this create a distance between grandmother and granddaughter?

4. Reread paragraphs 17–21 of the story. Which paragraphs suggest that Connie still doesn't fully realize how much her behavior has hurt her grandmother? Cite textual evidence that supports your answer.

5. Explain how Connie considers herself to be before Abuela comes to visit, and how this opinion changes by the end of the story. Cite textual evidence to support your response.

✏ WRITE

NARRATIVE: Write a letter that continues the story in which Constancia apologizes to Abuela and resolves the conflict between them. In your letter, include an example of Connie's responses to a decision or incident. In connection to the story's central idea or theme, explain what Connie has learned and how she has changed.

Inside Out & Back Again

FICTION
Thanhhà Lai
2011

Introduction

In many ways, the first novel by Thanhhà Lai (b. 1965) mirrors her own childhood experience. Like the main character, Hà, in *Inside Out & Back Again*, Thanhhà Lai witnessed the harsh reality of the Vietnam War, had a father who was missing in action, and fled with her family to America. Through Hà's character, Lai captures many of the universal feelings refugees experience in an unfamiliar place. In the four excerpts here, written in verse as first-person journal entries, Hà feels a rush of emotions as she repeats the fourth grade in her new home—Alabama.

"Deep breaths.
I'm the first student in class."

The Outside

NOTES

1 Starting tomorrow
2 everyone must
3 leave the house.

4 Mother starts sewing
5 at a factory;
6 Brother Quang begins
7 repairing cars.

8 The rest of us
9 must go to school,
10 repeating the last grade,
11 left unfinished.

12 Brother Vũ wants
13 to be a cook
14 or teach martial arts,
15 not waste a year
16 as the oldest senior.

17 Mother says
18 one word:
19 *College*.

20 Brother Khôi
21 gets an old bicycle to ride,
22 but Mother says
23 I'm too young for one
24 even though I'm
25 a ten-year-old
26 in the fourth grade,
27 when everyone else
28 is nine.

29 Mother says,
30 *Worry instead*
31 *about getting sleep*
32 *because from now on*
33 *no more naps.*
34 *You will eat lunch*
35 *at school*
36 *with friends.*

37 *What friends?*

38 *You'll make some.*

39 *What if I can't?*

40 *You will.*

41 *What will I eat?*

42 *What your friends eat.*

43 *But what will I eat?*

44 *Be surprised.*

45 *I hate surprises.*

46 *Be agreeable.*

47 *Not without knowing*
48 *what I'm agreeing to.*

49 Mother sighs,
50 walking away.

September 1

Sadder Laugh

51 School!

52 I wake up with
53 dragonflies
54 zipping through
55 my gut.

56   I eat nothing.

57   Mother shakes her head.

58   I take each step toward school evenly,
59   trying to hold my stomach
60   steady.

61   It helps that
62   the morning air glides cool
63   like a constant washcloth
64   against my face.

65   Deep breaths.

66   I'm the first student in class.

67   My new teacher has brown curls
68   looped tight to her scalp
69   like circles in a beehive.

70   She points to her chest:
71   *MiSSS SScott,*
72   saying it three times,
73   each louder
74   with ever more spit.

75   I repeat, *MiSSS SScott,*
76   careful to hiss every *s.*

77   She doesn't seem **impressed.**
78   I tap my own chest: *Hà.*

79   She must have heard *ha,*
80   as in funny *ha-ha-ha.*

81   She fakes a laugh.

82   I repeat, *Hà,*
83   and wish I knew
84   enough English
85   to tell her
86   to listen for
87   the **diacritical** mark,
88   this one directing
89   the tone

90 downward.

91 My new teacher
92 tilts her head back,
93 fakes
94 an even sadder laugh.

September 2
Morning

Rainbow

95 I face the class.
96 MiSSS SScott speaks.
97 Each classmate says something.

98 I don't understand,
99 but I see.

100 Fire hair on skin dotted with spots.
101 Fuzzy dark hair on skin shiny as **lacquer.**
102 Hair the color of root on milky skin.
103 Lots of braids on milk chocolate.
104 White hair on a pink boy.
105 Honey hair with orange ribbons on see-through skin.
106 Hair with barrettes in all colors on bronze bread.

107 I'm the only
108 straight black hair
109 on olive skin.

September 2
Midmorning

Black and White and Yellow and Red

110 The bell rings.
111 Everyone stands.
112 I stand.

113 They line up;
114 so do I.

115 Down a hall.
116 Turn left.
117 Take a tray.

118 Receive food.
119 Sit.

120 On one side
121 of the bright, noisy room,
122 light skin.
123 Other side,
124 dark skin.

125 Both laughing, chewing,
126 as if it never occurred
127 to them
128 someone **medium**
129 would show up.

130 I don't know where to sit
131 any more than
132 I know how to eat
133 the pink sausage
134 snuggled inside bread
135 shaped like a corncob,
136 **smeared** with sauces
137 yellow and red.

138 I think
139 they are making fun
140 of the Vietnamese flag[1]
141 until I remember
142 no one here likely knows
143 that flag's colors.

144 I put down the tray
145 and wait
146 in the hallway.

September 2
11:30 am

1. **Vietnamese flag** until 1975, the South Vietnamese flag consisted of a yellow background with three horizontal red stripes

WRITE

PERSONAL NARRATIVE: Hà doesn't know much English, so she describes her surroundings based on how she sees them. For example, she doesn't know what a hot dog is and describes it as "the pink sausage / snuggled inside bread / shaped like a corncob, / smeared with sauces / yellow and red." Choose a place from your own life—your classroom, the hallways, the library, your school's lunchroom— and describe it avoiding terms usually associated with the thing you describe. As you write your description, use the excerpt from *Inside Out and Back Again* as inspiration.

Theories of Time and Space

POETRY
Natasha Trethewey
2006

Introduction

Natasha Trethewey (b. 1966) has been a State Poet Laureate of Mississippi and a United States Poet Laureate, and she has won a Pulitzer Prize. Her poems combine reflections about the history of African Americans in Mississippi with her own experience growing up biracial in the South. Trethewey wrote "Theories of Time and Space" as the introduction to her book of poems *Native Guard*. That title refers to the Louisiana Native Guards, a group of black Union soldiers who watched over imprisoned Confederate soldiers on Ship Island, off the coast of Mississippi. Like other poems in the collection, "Theories of Time and Space" takes readers on a tour of the American South, while pondering how the passage of time makes everything different than what came before.

"Everywhere you go will be somewhere you've never been."

1 You can get there from here, though
2 there's no going home.

3 Everywhere you go will be somewhere
4 you've never been. Try this:

5 head south on Mississippi 49, one-
6 by-one mile markers ticking off

7 another minute of your life. Follow this
8 to its natural **conclusion**—dead end

9 at the coast, the pier at Gulfport where
10 riggings[1] of shrimp boats are loose stitches

11 in a sky threatening rain. Cross over
12 the man-made beach, 26 miles of sand

13 dumped on the mangrove[2] swamp—buried
14 **terrain** of the past. Bring only

15 what you must carry—**tome** of memory,
16 its random blank pages. On the dock

17 where you board the boat for Ship Island,
18 someone will take your picture:

19 the photograph—who you were—
20 will be waiting when you return.

---

1. **riggings** ropes used to operate sails aboard a ship
2. **mangrove** a type of tropical tree and shrub

NOTES

✏ WRITE

POETRY: "Theories of Time and Space" seems to be about a journey, more specifically the speaker's personal rules of the road. Imagine that you, like the speaker, go on a journey of your own. What do you see? What do you record in your "tome of memory"? Write a poem in any style to express your journey.

Please note that excerpts and passages in the StudySync® library and this workbook are intended as touchstones to generate interest in an author's work. The excerpts and passages do not substitute for the reading of entire texts, and StudySync® strongly recommends that students seek out and purchase the whole literary or informational work in order to experience it as the author intended. Links to online resellers are available in our digital library. In addition, complete works may be ordered through an authorized reseller by filling out and returning to StudySync® the order form enclosed in this workbook.

Reading & Writing Companion   **67**

The Road Not Taken

POETRY
Robert Frost
1915

Introduction

Robert Frost (1874–1963) was a United States Poet Laureate, and his poetry earned him four Pulitzer Prizes. Frost's classic poem "The Road Not Taken" is often interpreted as a nod to non-conformism, but some see it differently. When asked about the sigh in the last stanza, Frost wrote a friend, "It was my rather private jest at the expense of those who might think I would yet live to be sorry for

"Two roads diverged in a wood, and I—
I took the one less traveled by"

1 Two roads **diverged** in a yellow wood,
2 And sorry I could not travel both
3 And be one traveler, long I stood
4 And looked down one as far as I could
5 To where it bent in the **undergrowth;**

6 Then took the other, as just as fair[1],
7 And having perhaps the better **claim,**
8 Because it was grassy and wanted wear;
9 Though as for that the passing there
10 Had worn them really about the same,

11 And both that morning equally lay
12 In leaves no step had **trodden** black.
13 Oh, I kept the first for another day!
14 Yet knowing how way leads on to way,
15 I doubted if I should ever come back.

16 I shall be telling this with a sigh
17 Somewhere ages and ages **hence:**
18 Two roads diverged in a wood, and I—
19 I took the one less traveled by,
20 And that has made all the difference.

NOTES

**Skill:
Figurative
Language**

The speaker comes across two roads. He wants to take them both, but that's impossible. He has to make a choice. Along with the title, I think the purpose of these lines might be to introduce an extended metaphor about making choices.

**Skill:
Poetic Elements
and Structure**

Like the speaker in "Theories of Time and Space," the speaker here is also concerned with time and space.

Fork in the road

1. **fair** sufficient

Copyright © BookheadEd Learning, LLC

Reading & Writing Companion

First Read

Read "The Road Not Taken." After you read, complete the Think Questions below.

☁ **THINK QUESTIONS**

1. What evidence in the text of the poem shows you that the speaker is uncertain about which road to choose? Cite evidence from the text to support your answer.

2. What do lines 16–20 tell you about how the speaker imagines his future? Use evidence from the text to support your answer.

3. How does the speaker feel about the road he didn't take? Cite evidence from the text to support your answer.

4. Read the following dictionary entry:

   claim
   claim \ klām \ *noun*

   1. a demand or request for something that is owed
   2. a statement that you have a right to something
   3. a piece of land that is owned by someone

   Which definition most closely matches the meaning of **claim** as it is used in line 7 of "The Road Not Taken"? Write the correct definition of *claim* here, and explain how you figured out the correct meaning

5. Find the word **hence** in line 17 of "The Road Not Taken." Use context clues in the surrounding lines, as well as the line in which the word appears, to determine the word's meaning. Write your definition here and identify clues that helped you figure out its meaning.

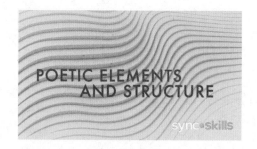

Skill:
Poetic Elements and Structure

Use the Checklist to analyze Poetic Elements and Structure in "The Road Not Taken." Refer to the sample student annotations about Poetic Elements and Structure in the text.

••• CHECKLIST FOR POETIC ELEMENTS AND STRUCTURE

In order to determine how to compare and contrast the structures of two or more poems, look for the following:

- ✓ the forms and overall structures of the poems

- ✓ the rhyme, rhythm, and meter, if present

- ✓ lines and stanzas in the poems that suggest the poems' meanings and styles

- ✓ ways that the poems' structures connect to the poems' meanings

To compare and contrast the structures of two or more poems and analyze how the differing structure of each text contributes to its meaning and style, consider the following questions:

- ✓ What forms do the poets use?

- ✓ How do the poems compare to each other in their structures?

- ✓ How does the choice of form or structure affect the overall meaning of each poem?

- ✓ How do the meanings of each poem compare?

Please note that excerpts and passages in the StudySync® library and this workbook are intended as touchstones to generate interest in an author's work. The excerpts and passages do not substitute for the reading of entire texts, and StudySync® strongly recommends that students seek out and purchase the whole literary or informational work in order to experience it as the author intended. Links to online resellers are available in our digital library. In addition, complete works may be ordered through an authorized reseller by filling out and returning to StudySync® the order form enclosed in this workbook.

Reading & Writing Companion

71

Skill:
Poetic Elements and Structure

Reread lines 9–14 of "Theories of Time and Space" and lines 11–15 of "The Road Not Taken." Then, using the Checklist on the previous page, complete the chart below to compare and contrast the passages.

⟳ YOUR TURN

	Observation Options
A	Poem has a structured rhyme scheme and meter.
B	Poem has no rhyme scheme or meter.
C	The structure helps communicate the way that man has negatively affected the natural world.
D	Both the narrators are influenced by the world as they encounter it.
E	Both poems have consistent line length.
F	The structure helps to communicate the beauty of nature.

"Theories of Time and Space"	Both	"The Road Not Taken"

Skill:
Figurative Language

Use the Checklist to analyze Figurative Language in "The Road Not Taken." Refer to the sample student annotations about Figurative Language in the text.

••• CHECKLIST FOR FIGURATIVE LANGUAGE

To determine the meaning of figures of speech in a text, note the following:

- ✓ words that mean one thing literally but suggest something else

- ✓ similes, such as "strong as an ox"

- ✓ metaphors, such as "her eyes were stars"

- ✓ analogies, or comparisons of two unlike things based on a specific similarity, used for clarification

  - remarking, "Life is like a ball game; anybody can have a losing day."

  - in Shakespeare's Sonnet 18, "Shall I compare thee to a summer's day? / Thou art more lovely and more temperate."

- ✓ extended metaphors, which make an implied comparison through the entirety of a text

In order to interpret the meaning of a figure of speech in context, ask the following questions:

- ✓ Does any of the descriptive language in the text compare two seemingly unlike things?

- ✓ Do any descriptions include *like* or *as*, indicating a simile?

- ✓ Is there a direct comparison that suggests a metaphor?

Please note that excerpts and passages in the StudySync® library and this workbook are intended as touchstones to generate interest in an author's work. The excerpts and passages do not substitute for the reading of entire texts, and StudySync® strongly recommends that students seek out and purchase the whole literary or informational work in order to experience it as the author intended. Links to online resellers are available in our digital library. In addition, complete works may be ordered through an authorized reseller by filling out and returning to StudySync® the order form enclosed in this workbook.

Reading & Writing
Companion

73

Skill:
Figurative Language

Reread lines 6–10 of "The Road Not Taken." Then, using the Checklist on the previous page, answer the multiple-choice questions below.

⟳ YOUR TURN

1. Based on the descriptive details in lines 6–8, the reader can conclude that—

   ○ A. Both roads are equally worthy of being chosen.

   ○ B. The second road is longer than the first road.

   ○ C. Fewer people choose to travel down the second road.

   ○ D. The first road is paved, but the second road is not.

2. Lines 6–10 best contribute to the extended metaphor in the poem by—

   ○ A. suggesting that there are no "right" choices in life.

   ○ B. showing that people make choices with the information they have.

   ○ C. introducing the idea that decisions are not important.

   ○ D. hinting that everyone ends up in the same place no matter what road they take.

Close Read

Reread "The Road Not Taken." As you reread, complete the Skills Focus questions below. Then use your answers and annotations from the questions to help you complete the Write activity.

◎ SKILLS FOCUS

1. Reread the first stanza of "The Road Not Taken," and look for clues that reveal the poem's structure. Identify a line or lines that contain elements that build that structure, such as rhyme, meter, or other elements. Then explain how the poet's choice to use such a structure helps him develop the meaning that life is a journey.

2. Reread the third stanza of "The Road Not Taken." Identify a detail that develops the extended metaphor in the poem, and explain the idea it communicates about making choices. Cite evidence from the poem to support your answer.

3. "The Road Not Taken," *Inside Out & Back Again*, and "Theories of Time and Space" each deal with the idea of turning points in our lives. Identify details in "The Road Not Taken" that reveal the speaker's thoughts on the turning point he faces. Explain how his thoughts are similar to or different from Hà's in *Inside Out & Back Again* and the speaker's in "Theories of Time and Space." Use specific evidence from the text(s) to support your claims.

4. The speaker of the poem implies that both roads are actually very similar. If that is true, then what is the significance of choosing one over the other? Which road would you choose and why? Use specific evidence from the text to support your claims.

✏ WRITE

POETRY: Think about a time you had to make an important choice. Write a poem to show the journey and the risk involved in that experience, as well as how it changed you. Your poem may use regular rhyme and meter or be in free verse, may be humorous or serious, and should include figurative language to develop ideas. Include a final line that states the poem's theme as it relates to your speaker and the events.

Please note that excerpts and passages in the StudySync® library and this workbook are intended as touchstones to generate interest in an author's work. The excerpts and passages do not substitute for the reading of entire texts, and StudySync® strongly recommends that students seek out and purchase the whole literary or informational work in order to experience it as the author intended. Links to online resellers are available in our digital library. In addition, complete works may be ordered through an authorized reseller by filling out and returning to StudySync® the order form enclosed in this workbook.

Reading & Writing Companion   75

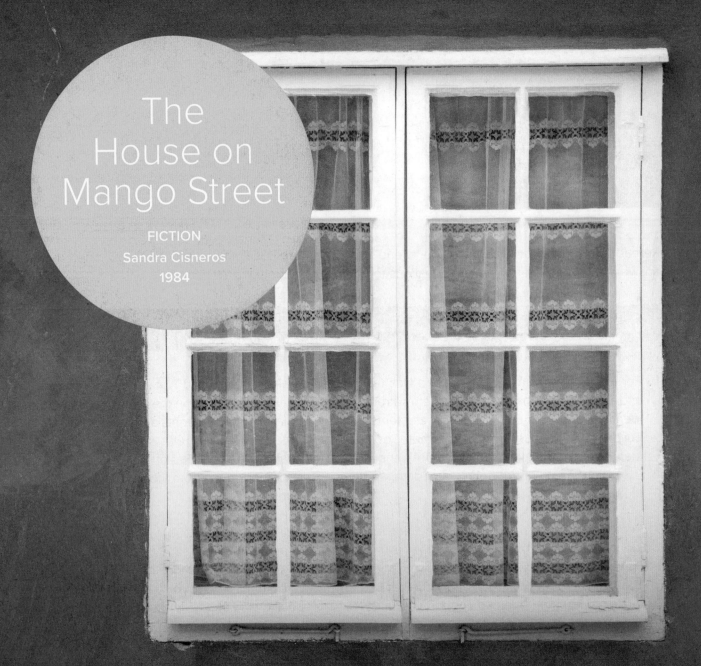

The House on Mango Street

FICTION
Sandra Cisneros
1984

Introduction

S andra Cisneros (b. 1954) is regarded as a prominent writer in the Chicana
literary movement. She has won numerous awards, including the National
Medal of Arts and the National Book Award. Her first novel, *The House on
Mango Street*, is a series of compressed, lyrical vignettes which center around a
Latina girl growing up in a Chicago barrio. From her little red house, the protagonist
Esperanza describes her life and the neighborhood around her. In this excerpt,
Esperanza gives readers a glimpse into her dissatisfaction with the present and her

"I have inherited her name, but I don't want to inherit her place by the window."

The House on Mango Street

1   They always told us that one day we would move into a house, a real house that would be ours for always so we wouldn't have to move each year. And our house would have running water and pipes that worked. And inside it would have real stairs, not hallway stairs, but stairs inside like the houses on TV. And we'd have a basement and at least three washrooms so when we took a bath we wouldn't have to tell everybody. Our house would be white with trees around it, a great big yard and grass growing without a fence. This was the house Papa talked about when he held a lottery ticket and this was the house Mama dreamed up in the stories she told us before we went to bed.

2   But the house on Mango Street is not the way they told it at all. It's small and red with tight steps in front and windows so small you'd think they were holding their breath. Bricks are crumbling in places, and the front door is so swollen you have to push hard to get in. There is no front yard, only four little elms the city planted by the curb. Out back is a small garage for the car we don't own yet and a small yard that looks smaller between the two buildings on either side. There are stairs in our house, but they're ordinary hallway stairs, and the house has only one washroom. Everybody has to share a bedroom—Mama and Papa, Carlos and Kiki, me and Nenny.

3   Once when we were living on Loomis, a nun[1] from my school passed by and saw me playing out front. The **laundromat** downstairs had been boarded up because it had been robbed two days before and the owner had painted on the wood YES WE'RE OPEN so as not to lose business.

4   Where do you live? she asked.

5   There, I said pointing up to the third floor.

6   You live *there*?

---

1. **nun** a female member of a religious order, often the staff and faculty at Catholic schools

Skill:
Figurative
Language

The description of windows "so small you'd think they were holding their breath" is an example of personification. I can picture windows sucking in their breath, so small they can't let any air out even when they're open.

Reading & Writing Companion   **77**

7 *There.* I had to look to where she pointed—the third floor, the paint peeling, wooden bars Papa had nailed on the windows so we wouldn't fall out. You live *there?* The way she said it made me feel like nothing. *There.* I lived *there.* I nodded.

8 I knew then I had to have a house. A real house. One I could point to. But this isn't it. The house on Mango Street isn't it. For the time being, Mama says. Temporary, says Papa. But I know how those things go.

· · ·

My Name

Skill:
Figurative
Language

The metaphor "a wild horse of a woman" doesn't use *like* or *as.* This communicates that the author's great-grandmother was independent. The simile "as if she were a fancy chandelier" implies how valuable she was to her great-grandfather.

9 In English my name means hope. In Spanish it means too many letters. It means sadness, it means waiting. It is like the number nine. A muddy color. It is the Mexican records my father plays on Sunday mornings when he is shaving, songs like sobbing.

10 It was my great-grandmother's name and now it is mine. She was a horse woman too, born like me in the Chinese year of the horse—which is supposed to be bad luck if you're born female—but I think this is a Chinese lie because the Chinese, like the Mexicans, don't like their women strong.

11 My great-grandmother. I would've liked to have known her, a wild horse of a woman, so wild she wouldn't marry. Until my great-grandfather threw a sack over her head and carried her off. Just like that, as if she were a fancy **chandelier**. That's the way he did it.

12 And the story goes she never forgave him. She looked out the window her whole life, the way so many women sit their sadness on an elbow. I wonder if she made the best with what she got or was she sorry because she couldn't be all the things she wanted to be. Esperanza. I have inherited her name, but I don't want to **inherit** her place by the window.

13 At school they say my name funny as if the syllables were made out of tin and hurt the roof of your mouth. But in Spanish my name is made out of a softer something, like silver, not quite as thick as sister's name—Magdalena—which is uglier than mine. Magdalena who at least can come home and become Nenny. But I am always Esperanza.

14 I would like to **baptize** myself under a new name, a name more like the real me, the one nobody sees. Esperanza as Lisandra or Maritza or Zeze the X. Yes. Something like Zeze the X will do.

· · ·

Skill:
Summarizing

Esperanza wants to be her own person instead of having a name related to her heritage. She wants to separate herself from her parents and sister. Changing her name seems to her an important step in that direction.

Please note that excerpts and passages in the StudySync® library and this workbook are intended as touchstones to generate interest in an author's work. The excerpts and passages do not substitute for the reading of entire texts, and StudySync® strongly recommends that students seek out and purchase the whole literary or informational work in order to experience it as the author intended. Links to online resellers are available in our digital library. In addition, complete works may be ordered through an authorized reseller by filling out and returning to StudySync® the order form enclosed in this workbook.

Four Skinny Trees

15   They are the only ones who understand me. I am the only one who understands them. Four skinny trees with skinny necks and pointy elbows like mine. Four who do not belong here but are here. Four raggedy excuses planted by the city. From our room we can hear them, but Nenny just sleeps and doesn't appreciate these things.

16   Their strength is secret. They send **ferocious** roots beneath the ground. They grow up and they grow down and grab the earth between their hairy toes and bite the sky with violent teeth and never quit their anger. This is how they keep.

17   Let one forget his reason for being, they'd all droop like tulips in a glass, each with their arms around the other. Keep, keep, keep, trees say when I sleep. They teach.

Excerpted from *The House on Mango Street* by Sandra Cisneros, published by Vintage Books.

First Read

Read *The House on Mango Street*. After you read, complete the Think Questions below.

1. How is the family's dream house different from their real house on Mango Street? Cite evidence from the selection to support your answer.

2. How does Esperanza's encounter with the nun affect her? Explain how she feels after this brief encounter. Cite evidence from the text.

3. Why do you think Esperanza identifies with the four skinny trees outside her window? What does this tell you about her? Cite evidence from the text.

4. Read the following dictionary entry:

   inherit
   in•her•it \in 'her it\ *verb*

   1. to receive money or property from someone who has died
   2. to receive a genetic trait from a parent or ancestor
   3. to have something, such as a job or attitude, after someone who came before you

   Which definition most closely matches the meaning of **inherit** as it is used in paragraph 12? Write the appropriate definition of *inherit* here and explain how you figured out the correct meaning.

5. Find the word **ferocious** in paragraph 16 of *The House on Mango Street*. Use context clues in the surrounding sentences, as well as the sentence in which the word appears, to determine the word's meaning. Write your definition here and identify clues that helped you figure out its meaning.

Skill:
Figurative Language

Use the Checklist to analyze Figurative Language in *The House on Mango Street*. Refer to the sample student annotations about Figurative Language in the text.

••• CHECKLIST FOR FIGURATIVE LANGUAGE

To determine the meaning of figurative language in a text, note the following:

✓ words that mean one thing literally but suggest something else

✓ similes, such as "strong as an ox," or metaphors, such as "her eyes were stars"

✓ the use of personification, which gives human traits and qualities to something nonhuman, such as "the flowers smiled at us as we walked through the garden"

✓ puns, or plays on words, such as saying, "Let's branch out," while walking in the woods with friends

In order to interpret the meaning of a figure of speech in context, ask the following questions:

✓ How does descriptive language in the text compare two seemingly unlike things?

✓ Are there any similes or metaphors in the text? How do you know?

✓ Are there any examples of personification?

✓ Do you see any words that have two meanings that are used deliberately for humor or a pun?

✓ How does the use of figurative language change your understanding of the thing or person being described?

In order to analyze the impact of figurative language on the meaning of a text, use the following questions as a guide:

✓ Where does figurative language appear in the text? What does it mean?

✓ What impact do specific word choices have on meaning and tone, or the writer's attitude toward the subject or audience?

Please note that excerpts and passages in the StudySync® library and this workbook are intended as touchstones to generate interest in an author's work. The excerpts and passages do not substitute for the reading of entire texts, and StudySync® strongly recommends that students seek out and purchase the whole literary or informational work in order to experience it as the author intended. Links to online resellers are available in our digital library. In addition, complete works may be ordered through an authorized reseller by filling out and returning to StudySync® the order form enclosed in this workbook.

Reading & Writing Companion   **81**

Skill:
Figurative Language

Reread paragraphs 15–17 of *The House on Mango Street*. Then, using the Checklist on the previous page, answer the multiple-choice questions below.

⟳ YOUR TURN

1. The personification in paragraph 15 helps show that—

   ○ A. Esperanza thinks the trees are dying.

   ○ B. Esperanza feels annoyed by the trees.

   ○ C. Esperanza feels a connection to the trees.

   ○ D. Esperanza is the only person who sees the trees.

2. The personification in paragraph 16 helps communicate that the trees are—

   ○ A. weak.

   ○ B. aging.

   ○ C. strong.

   ○ D. dangerous.

3. The simile in paragraph 17 helps the reader understand—

   ○ A. defeat.

   ○ B. support.

   ○ C. strength.

   ○ D. determination.

Skill:
Summarizing

Use the Checklist to analyze Summarizing in *The House on Mango Street*. Refer to the sample student annotations about Summarizing in the text.

In order to determine how to write an objective summary of a text, note the following:

✓ in a nonfiction text, examine the details to identify the main idea, making notations in a notebook or graphic organizer

✓ in literature, note the setting, characters, and events in the plot and their relationship to the theme

✓ answers to the basic questions *who, what, where, when, why,* and *how*

✓ stay objective, and do not add your own personal thoughts, judgments, or opinions to the summary

To provide an objective summary of a text, consider the following questions:

✓ What are the answers to basic *who, what, where, when, why,* and *how* questions in literature and works of nonfiction?

✓ In what order should I put the main ideas and most important details in a work of nonfiction to make my summary logical?

✓ In a work of literature, have I included details that reflect the relationship of the setting, characters, and events in the plot to the theme?

✓ Is my summary objective, or have I added my own thoughts, judgments, and personal opinions?

Skill:
Summarizing

Reread paragraphs 9–12 of *The House on Mango Street*. Then, using the Checklist on the previous page, answer the multiple-choice questions below.

⟳ YOUR TURN

1. This question has two parts. First, answer Part A. Then, answer Part B.

   Part A: Which of the following is the theme or central idea of this passage?

   ○ A. A person's identity is defined by the name that he or she was given.

   ○ B. Every person has a story to tell about their names.

   ○ C. Esperanza's name makes her unique.

   ○ D. A name can influence a person's identity.

   Part B: How does the character relate to the theme you selected in Part A?

   ○ A. Esperanza's name is both a source of strength and a concern for her.

   ○ B. Esperanza thinks that she has no control over her future because of her name.

   ○ C. Esperanza shares the story behind her name and wants to learn the story behind her father's name.

   ○ D. Esperanza thinks that her name shows that she is different from everyone else.

2. Summarize Esperanza's feelings about her great-grandmother.

   ○ A. She seems to think she was weak.

   ○ B. She seems to like her because, like her great-grandmother, Esperanza was born in the Chinese year of the horse.

   ○ C. She seems to admire her, describing in detail her great-grandmother's independent streak, but at the same time does not want to inherit her sadness.

   ○ D. She seems to dislike her because she was sad all the time.

 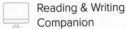

3. During this passage, Esperanza mentions some reasons why she doesn't like her name. Summarize her feelings towards her name.

- ○ A. Esperanza dislikes her name for many reasons, including that it means "sadness" and "waiting" and has too many letters.
- ○ B. Esperanza dislikes her name because it means "hope" in English.
- ○ C. Esperanza dislikes her name because it reminds her of the sad records her father plays while he is shaving.
- ○ D. Esperanza likes names that contain fewer syllables.

Please note that excerpts and passages in the StudySync® library and this workbook are intended as touchstones to generate interest in an author's work. The excerpts and passages do not substitute for the reading of entire texts, and StudySync® strongly recommends that students seek out and purchase the whole literary or informational work in order to experience it as the author intended. Links to online resellers are available in our digital library. In addition, complete works may be ordered through an authorized reseller by filling out and returning to StudySync® the order form enclosed in this workbook.

Reading & Writing
Companion

85

Close Read

Reread *The House on Mango Street*. As you reread, complete the Skills Focus questions below. Then use your answers and annotations from the questions to help you complete the Write activity.

◎ SKILLS FOCUS

1. Provide a descriptive summary of Esperanza's feelings toward the house on Mango Street. Include as many relevant details as possible, being sure to cite the text when necessary.

2. Identify the figurative language in paragraph 9 of the excerpt from *The House on Mango Street*. Explain what ideas Esperanza is expressing through her use of figurative language.

3. Identify the figurative language in paragraph 13 of the excerpt from *The House on Mango Street*. Explain how the figurative comparison helps the reader understand how Esperanza feels.

4. Summarize Esperanza's thoughts about the trees. What do they seem to represent to her, and why are they significant enough to be a focal point within her narrative?

5. Like many others, Esperanza struggles with who she is. Identify examples of this struggle and explain what makes the narrator uncomfortable. Be sure to emphasize how coming to terms with one's identity is an important part of determining what makes someone themselves.

✏ WRITE

ARGUMENTATIVE: Esperanza faces several internal and external struggles. **Overall**, what are Esperanza's biggest challenges? Summarize the challenges Esperanza faces in each section of the text, and explain how figurative language is used to convey those challenges. Be sure to support your ideas with evidence from the text.

Extended
Writing
Project and
Grammar

EXTENDED
WRITING
PROJECT
LITERARY ANALYSIS
WRITING

Literary Analysis Writing Process: Plan

PLAN	DRAFT	REVISE	EDIT AND PUBLISH

It's not always easy to define who we are. However, many of this unit's authors use metaphors to communicate an individual's perspective on his or her identity or sense of belonging. In *The House on Mango Street*, Esperanza describes her name by saying, "It is the Mexican records my father plays on Sunday mornings when he is shaving, songs like sobbing." In the poem "Slam, Dunk, & Hook," the speaker artfully describes how he and his friends play in sync during a basketball game: "Our bodies spun / On swivels of bone & faith." In the story "Abuela Invents the Zero," Abuela also uses a metaphor to express what it feels like to be rejected by a family member: "You made me feel like a zero, like a nothing."

WRITING PROMPT

What is the power of a metaphor?

Examine the texts from this unit and select three powerful metaphors that deepen our understanding of identity and belonging. Your analysis should explain each metaphor and make an argument about how the metaphor reveals something about each speaker, character, or author. Be sure your literary analysis includes the following:

- an introduction
- a claim
- coherent body paragraphs
- reasons and relevant evidence
- a formal style

Writing to Sources

As you gather ideas and information from the texts, or sources, in the unit, be sure to:

- include a claim about each one;
- use evidence from each one; and
- avoid overly relying on one text or source.

Introduction to Argumentative Writing

An argumentative essay is a form of persuasive writing where the writer makes a claim about a topic and then provides evidence—facts, details, examples, and quotations—to convince readers to accept and agree with the writer's claim. In order to provide convincing supporting evidence for an argumentative essay, the writer must often do outside research as well as cite the sources of the evidence that is presented in the essay.

A literary analysis is a form of argumentative writing that tries to persuade readers to accept the writer's interpretation of a literary text. Good literary analysis writing builds an argument with a strong claim, convincing reasons, relevant textual evidence, and a clear structure with an introduction, body, and conclusion. The characteristics of argumentative and literary analysis writing include:

- introduction
- claim
- thesis statement
- textual evidence
- transitions
- formal style
- conclusion

As you continue with this Extended Writing Project, you'll receive more instruction and practice at crafting each of the characteristics of argumentative writing to create your own literary analysis.

Please note that excerpts and passages in the StudySync® library and this workbook are intended as touchstones to generate interest in an author's work. The excerpts and passages do not substitute for the reading of entire texts, and StudySync® strongly recommends that students seek out and purchase the whole literary or informational work in order to experience it as the author intended. Links to online resellers are available in our digital library. In addition, complete works may be ordered through an authorized reseller by filling out and returning to StudySync® the order form enclosed in this workbook.

Reading & Writing
Companion

89

Before you get started on your own literary analysis, read this literary analysis that one student, Donovan, wrote in response to the writing prompt. As you read the Model, highlight and annotate the features of argumentative writing that Donovan included in his narrative.

NOTES

☰ STUDENT MODEL

What's in a Name? How Metaphors Can Express Identity

1 *Who are you?* At first this question seems easy. A person might answer it by saying his or her name. However, a name is just one small part of a person's identity. Identity includes memories, goals, thoughts, and actions. While one could argue that those aspects of a person can never be captured in writing, authors can use figurative language to reveal complex parts of a character's unique identity. In the excerpts from *The House on Mango Street*, the main character's name is a metaphor for how she feels about the world around her. Likewise, in the poem "Slam, Dunk, & Hook," the game of basketball, a labyrinth, and a sea monster are used to act as metaphors for a strong community. They drastically differ from the metaphor that Abuela uses in "Abuela Invents the Zero." In that story, the number zero is used by Abuela to express how it feels to be excluded by a group. Each one of these metaphors helps readers see how a character's community can influence his or her identity.

2 In *The House on Mango Street*, Esperanza uses her name as a metaphor for the way she sees herself and her place in her community. Esperanza's name is defined in this selection, and she also defines what it means to her: "In English my name means hope. In Spanish it means too many letters. It means sadness, it means waiting. It is like the number nine. A muddy color" (paragraph 9). As a reflection of her name, Esperanza does have some hope that her parents will purchase a house that they have promised her. She thinks that a better home might make her feel more proud about her place in the community. Even if that dream were to come true, however, Esperanza would still see her own name as a barrier to belonging. This is evident when she says, "At school they say my name funny as if the syllables were made out of tin and hurt the roof of your mouth" (paragraph 13). Esperanza's name is a major part of her identity, so she feels out of place when her classmates struggle with it. In this excerpt, she even wants to change her name to solve

the problem. As a result, her name acts as a metaphor, and it holds more than one meaning in this selection. It shows her desire to belong to a community and the difficulty of doing that.

3   Like Esperanza, the speaker in the poem "Slam, Dunk, & Hook" wants to connect with other people. In the poem, the speaker and his friends create a strong community based on basketball. In fact, the speaker even speaks on behalf of the group by using the pronouns *we* and *our* instead of *I* throughout the poem. These pronouns emphasize that the speaker is describing experiences he has shared with his friends. He also uses the metaphor of a labyrinth to show how strong every member of the group feels when they play basketball together: "In the roundhouse / Labyrinth our bodies / Created, we could almost / Last forever, poised in midair / Like storybook sea monsters" (lines 7–10). The metaphor shows that the speaker and his friends feel invincible when they play. A labyrinth is a huge, complex maze, so the speaker's comparison suggests that their moves are highly developed and impressive. In addition, the comparison to "storybook sea monsters" shows that playing basketball makes the speaker and his friends feel as if they are tough competitors who are ready to destroy their opponents. One could argue that this excerpt includes "mixed metaphors," disconnected comparisons that sound like nonsense when strung together; however, they do have important connections. A labyrinth and a sea monster are both associated with myths and legends, so they imply that these friends have superhuman strength and endurance when they play together. Furthermore, a labyrinth and sea monster are made up of many parts that work together to create entities that can be "beautiful & dangerous," like this group of friends (line 40). Although there are multiple metaphors in this poem, they show readers that a strong community can help each member thrive.

4   As a contrast, the short story "Abuela Invents the Zero" shows how insignificant a person can feel when he or she does not conform to a community's expectations. In this story, Constancia and her family are visited by Abuela, and Constancia notices that her grandmother looks out of place everywhere they go. When they go to church, for example, she compares Abuela to the explorer Captain Cousteau, trying to make sense of a new underwater world. When Abuela has trouble finding her seat, Constancia then ignores her because she is

overwhelmed with embarrassment. After they return home, Abuela tells Constancia how she felt when Constancia failed to help her: "You made me feel like a zero, like a nothing" (paragraph 16). She uses a simile, a comparison that includes the words *like* or *as*, to express her feelings of worthlessness. The "Zero" in the story's title, "Abuela Invents the Zero," also shows how important this simile is. It suggests that Constancia does not realize how much neglect can hurt another person until her grandmother explains it. As a result, Abuela's simile shows the need to help relatives find ways to be a part of a community, even if that community is unfamiliar to them.

5   *The House on Mango Street*, "Slam, Dunk, & Hook," and "Abuela Invents the Zero" each use metaphor to show readers how community can affect a person's identity. In *The House on Mango Street*, Esperanza's name reveals a longing to feel like she belongs in her community. The speaker in "Slam, Dunk, & Hook" also offers a different perspective by using metaphors to illustrate how a person can find strength in community bonds. Under different circumstances, Constancia abandons her grandmother when she is lost in "Abuela Invents the Zero." Abuela then uses the number zero as a metaphor to explain how that disrespect made her feel. In each text, figurative language helps readers understand how a community can influence the way people see themselves.

✏ WRITE

Writers often take notes before they sit down to write. Think about what you've learned so far about literary analyses to help you begin prewriting.

- Which texts from the unit would you like to write about?

- How do the characters, narrators, speakers, or authors of those texts express their ideas about identity and belonging?

- What kind of figurative language do the characters, narrators, speakers, or authors use?

- How does that figurative language, including metaphor, help them communicate their ideas in a unique way?

- What kinds of textual evidence might you use to support your ideas?

- What kinds of transition words and phrases could you use to connect your ideas in a logical way?

Response Instructions

Use the questions in the bulleted list to write a one-paragraph summary. Your summary should identify the texts you want to write about and at least one idea about how the characters, speakers, or authors of those texts use metaphor and other figurative language to express themselves.

Don't worry about including all of the details now; focus only on the most essential and important elements. You will refer back to this short paragraph as you continue through the steps of the writing process.

Please note that excerpts and passages in the StudySync® library and this workbook are intended as touchstones to generate interest in an author's work. The excerpts and passages do not substitute for the reading of entire texts, and StudySync® strongly recommends that students seek out and purchase the whole literary or informational work in order to experience it as the author intended. Links to online resellers are available in our digital library. In addition, complete works may be ordered through an authorized reseller by filling out and returning to StudySync® the order form enclosed in this workbook.

Reading & Writing
Companion

93

Skill:
Organizing Argumentative Writing

Copyright © BookheadEd Learning, LLC

••• CHECKLIST FOR ORGANIZING ARGUMENTATIVE WRITING

As you consider how to organize your writing for your argumentative essay, use the following questions as a guide:

- What is my position on this topic?
- Have I chosen the best organizational structure to present my information logically?
- Have I acknowledged, or recognized, opposing claims and presented evidence to distinguish them from my own?
- Can my claim be supported by logical reasoning and relevant evidence?
- Do I have enough evidence to support my claim?

Follow these steps to plan out the organization of your argumentative essay, including organizing your reasons and evidence logically:

- Identify your claim.
  - > Write a statement that will present your claim in the first paragraph.
- Choose an organizational structure that will present your claim logically.
- Recognize claims that oppose or disagree with your claim, and present evidence that distinguishes your claim from others.
- Identify reasons and evidence that support your claim.
- Note that textual evidence can be proven to be true in other sources, and may be in the form of:
  - > numbers or statistics
  - > quotes from experts
  - > names or dates
  - > reference sources

YOUR TURN

Read the quotations from a student's argumentative essay called "Mirrors and Windows" below. Then, complete the chart by matching each quotation with its correct place in the outline.

	Quotations
A	To deepen their understanding of shared and diverse experiences, people need to read books that act like mirrors and books that act like windows.
B	Books that act like windows show readers cultural backgrounds, experiences, and challenges that are not familiar to them. They help readers learn about experiences that they have not had and see the world in new ways.
C	How can books act like mirrors and windows?
D	Books that act like mirrors show readers cultural backgrounds, experiences, and challenges that are familiar to them. They can help readers see their experiences in new ways.
E	One can argue that all good literature acts like a mirror and a window since it should include universal themes and unique perspectives. However, it is important to read books with characters from a wide range of backgrounds to learn about different cultures, struggles, and points of view.

Outline	Quotation
Introductory Statement:	
Thesis Statement:	
Main Idea 1:	
Main Idea 2:	
Main Idea 3:	

YOUR TURN

Complete the chart below by writing a short summary of what you will focus on in each section of your essay.

Outline	Summary
Introductory Statement:	
Thesis Statement:	
Main Idea 1:	
Main Idea 2:	
Main Idea 3:	

Reading & Writing Companion

Skill:
Thesis Statement

••• CHECKLIST FOR THESIS STATEMENT

Before you begin writing your thesis statement, ask yourself the following questions:

- What is the prompt asking me to write about?
- What is the topic of my essay? How can I state it clearly for the reader?
- What claim do I want to make about the topic of this essay? Is my opinion clear to my reader?
- Does my thesis statement introduce the body of my essay?
- Where should I place my thesis statement?

Here are some methods to introduce and develop your claim and topic clearly:

- Think about the topic and central idea of your essay.
  - > The central idea of an argument is stated as a claim, or what will be proven or shown to be true.
  - > Identify as many claims as you intend to prove.

- Write a clear statement about the central idea or claim. Your thesis statement should:
  - > let the reader anticipate the body of your essay
  - > respond completely to the writing prompt

- Consider the best placement for your thesis statement.
  - > If your response is short, you may want to get right to the point. Your thesis statement may be presented in the first sentence of the essay.
  - > If your response is longer (as in a formal essay), you can build up your thesis statement. In this case, you can place your thesis statement at the end of your introductory paragraph.

Please note that excerpts and passages in the StudySync® library and this workbook are intended as touchstones to generate interest in an author's work. The excerpts and passages do not substitute for the reading of entire texts, and StudySync® strongly recommends that students seek out and purchase the whole literary or informational work in order to experience it as the author intended. Links to online resellers are available in our digital library. In addition, complete works may be ordered through an authorized reseller by filling out and returning to StudySync® the order form enclosed in this workbook.

Reading & Writing Companion

97

⟳ YOUR TURN

Read the sentences below. Then, complete the chart by sorting them into those that are effective thesis statements and those that are not.

	Sentences
A	Shirley Jackson's "The Lottery" is set in a small town.
B	In "The Monkey's Paw," W. W. Jacobs warns readers about the perils of mocking superstition.
C	Walter Dean Myers's *Monster* shows that a person's environment can change the way they see themselves.
D	Walter Dean Myers's *Monster* is both a novel and a screenplay.
E	"The Lottery" serves as a warning against blindly following tradition without considering the consequences.
F	"The Monkey's Paw" is a suspenseful story.

Effective Thesis Statement	Ineffective Thesis Statement

✐ WRITE

Follow the steps in the checklist section to draft a thesis statement for your literary analysis.

Skill:
Reasons and Relevant Evidence

••• CHECKLIST FOR REASONS AND RELEVANT EVIDENCE

As you begin to determine what reasons and relevant evidence will support your claim(s), use the following questions as a guide:

- What is the claim (or claims) that I am making in my argument?

- What textual evidence am I using to support this claim? Is it relevant?

- Am I quoting the source accurately?

- Does my evidence display logical reasoning and relate to the claim I am making?

Use the following steps as a guide to help you determine how you will support your claim(s) with logical reasoning and relevant evidence, using accurate and credible sources:

- Identify the claim(s) you will make in your argument.

- Select evidence from credible sources that will convince others to accept your claim(s).

  > Look for reliable and relevant sources of information online, such as government or educational websites.

  > Search print resources such as books written by an expert or authority on a topic.

- Explain the connection between your claim(s) and the evidence selected in which you demonstrate an understanding of the topic or text.

- Think about whether your reasoning is logical and develops naturally from the evidence you have found to support your claim.

Please note that excerpts and passages in the StudySync® library and this workbook are intended as touchstones to generate interest in an author's work. The excerpts and passages do not substitute for the reading of entire texts, and StudySync® strongly recommends that students seek out and purchase the whole literary or informational work in order to experience it as the author intended. Links to online resellers are available in our digital library. In addition, complete works may be ordered through an authorized reseller by filling out and returning to StudySync® the order form enclosed in this workbook.

Reading & Writing
Companion

99

⟳ YOUR TURN

Read each piece of textual evidence from *The House on Mango Street* below. Then, complete the chart by sorting them into those that support Donovan's thesis statement and those that do not.

	Textual Evidence
A	You live *there*? The way she said it made me feel like nothing. *There*. I lived *there*.
B	Once when we were living on Loomis, a nun from my school passed by and saw me playing out front. The laundromat downstairs had been boarded up because it had been robbed two days before and the owner had painted on the wood YES WE'RE OPEN so as not to lose business.
C	This was the house Papa talked about when he held a lottery ticket and this was the house Mama dreamed up in the stories she told us before we went to bed.
D	The house on Mango Street isn't it. For the time being, Mama says. Temporary, says Papa.
E	They are the only ones who understand me. I am the only one who understands them. Four skinny trees with skinny necks and pointy elbows like mine. Four who do not belong here but are here.
F	In English my name means hope. In Spanish it means too many letters. It means sadness, it means waiting. It is like the number nine. A muddy color. It is the Mexican records my father plays on Sunday mornings when he is shaving, songs like sobbing.

Supports Thesis Statement	Does Not Support Thesis Statement

YOUR TURN

Complete the chart below by identifying textual evidence from each selection you've chosen that you can use to develop your own thesis statement.

Selection	Textual Evidence
Selection #1	
Selection #2	
Selection #3	

Literary Analysis Writing Process: Draft

PLAN	DRAFT	REVISE	EDIT AND PUBLISH

You have already made progress toward writing your literary analysis. Now it is time to draft your literary analysis.

✏ WRITE

Use your plan and other responses in your Binder to draft your literary analysis. You may also have new ideas as you begin drafting. Feel free to explore those new ideas as you have them. You can also ask yourself these questions:

- Have I stated my claim clearly?

- Have I supported my claim with logical reasons and relevant evidence?

- Does my organization make sense?

Before you submit your draft, read it over carefully. You want to be sure that you've responded to all aspects of the prompt.

Here is Donovan's literary analysis draft. There may be mistakes in the draft, but he can correct those later in the process. As you read, identify reasons and relevant evidence that develop the argument in his thesis statement.

STUDENT MODEL: FIRST DRAFT

What's In A Name? How Metaphors Can Express Identity

It can be hard to define who you are. In fiction, authors have to define their characters for readers. Characters' unique identities are shown through figurative language, such as metaphors. In *The House on Mango Street*, "Slam, Dunk, & Hook," and "Abuela Invents the Zero," metaphors show not only who the characters are, but why it is important to be part of a community.

Who are you? At first this question seems easy. A person might answer it by saying his or her name. However, a name is just one small part of a person's identity. Identity includes memories, goals, thoughts, and actions. While one could argue that those aspects of a person can never be captured in writing, authors can use figurative language to reveal complex parts of a character's unique identity. In the excerpts from *The House on Mango Street,* the main character's name is a metaphor for how she feels about the world around her. Likewise, in the poem "Slam, Dunk, & Hook," the game of basketball, a labyrinth, and a sea monster are used to act as metaphors for a strong community. They drastically differ from the metaphor that Abuela uses in "Abuela Invents the Zero." In that story, the number zero is used by Abuela to express how it feels to be excluded by a group. Each one of these metaphors helps readers see how a character's community can influence his or her identity.

When I read this part of *The House On Mango Street*, I saw that Esperanza uses her name to show her identity. It also shows that her relationship is connected to her community. Esperanza's name and what it means to her is defined in this selection: "In English my name means hope. In Spanish it means too many letters. It means sadness, it means waiting. It is like the number nine. A muddy color" (paragraph 9). You can see that Esperanza has some hope. She hopes that her parents will get a nice house. If they do, she can then have freinds over to hang out. There's no way that'll happen until

Skill:
Introductions

Donovan revises his paragraph to include an interesting hook, a preview of the argument that he will make in his essay, and a claim that clearly relates to the rest of the paragraph.

Please note that excerpts and passages in the StudySync® library and this workbook are intended as touchstones to generate interest in an author's work. The excerpts and passages do not substitute for the reading of entire texts, and StudySync® strongly recommends that students seek out and purchase the whole literary or informational work in order to experience it as the author intended. Links to online resellers are available in our digital library. In addition, complete works may be ordered through an authorized reseller by filling out and returning to StudySync® the order form enclosed in this workbook.

Reading & Writing Companion   **103**

NOTES

Skill:
Style

Donovan looks for ways to make the style more formal. He spells out contractions and removes slang terms like "hang out" and "never really be cool." He also replaces the first-person pronoun *I* and second-person pronoun *you* with third-person pronouns. Donovan replaces a phrase with the term *metaphor*, one example of academic language. To vary his sentences and avoid confusing readers, Donovan combines several shorter sentences into longer sentences that are easier to follow.

~~they get that house though. And even with the house, Esperanza would still never really be cool. She says, "At school they say my name funny as if the syllables were made out of tin and hurt the roof of your mouth" (paragraph 13). Like my name, Esperanza's name is a major part of her identity, so she feels out of place when her classmates can't say it. She even wants to change her name to solve the problem. Her name acts as a metaphor. It holds more than one meaning in this selection. It shows her desire to belong to a community and the difficulty of doing that.~~

In *The House on Mango Street*, Esperanza uses her name as a metaphor for the way she sees herself and her place in her community. Esperanza's name is defined in this selection, and she also defines what it means to her: "In English my name means hope. In Spanish it means too many letters. It means sadness, it means waiting. It is like the number nine. A muddy color" (paragraph 9). As a reflection of her name, Esperanza does have some hope that her parents will purchase a house that they have promised her. She thinks that a better home might make her feel more proud about her place in the community. Even if that dream were to come true, however, Esperanza would still see her own name as a barrier to belonging. This is evident when she says, "At school they say my name funny as if the syllables were made out of tin and hurt the roof of your mouth" (paragraph 13). Esperanza's name is a major part of her identity, so she feels out of place when her classmates struggle with it. In this excerpt, she even wants to change her name to solve the problem. As a result, her name acts as a metaphor, and it holds more than one meaning in this selection. It shows her desire to belong to a community and the difficulty of doing that.

Like Esperanza, the speaker in the poem "Slam, Dunk, & Hook" wants to connect with other people. In the poem, the speaker and his friends create a strong community based on basketball. The speaker even uses the pronouns we and *our* instead of *I* throughout the poem. The metaphors of a labyrinth and a sea monster also show how they feel when they play basketball together: "In the roundhouse / Labyrinth our bodies / Created, we could almost / Last forever, poised in midair / Like storybook sea monsters" (lines 7–10). The labyrinth and sea monster are made up of multiple parts that work together to create something that can be "beautiful &

dangerous," a phrase that is used by the speaker to describe his group of friends (line 40). Although there are multiple metaphors in this poem, they show readers that a strong community can help each member thrive.

~~The short story "Abuela Invents the Zero" shows how insignificant a person can feel when he or she does not try to conform with a community's expectations. When Abuela visits Constancia and her family, she notices that Abuela is out of place everywhere they go. They go to church. She compares Abuela to Captain Cousteau trying to make sense of a new underwater world. Instead of helping her grandmother figure out where to go, Constancia would ignore her, and Abuela ends up getting lost.~~

As a contrast, the short story "Abuela Invents the Zero" shows how insignificant a person can feel when he or she does not conform to a community's expectations. In this story, Constancia and her family are visited by Abuela, and Constancia notices that her grandmother looks out of place everywhere they go. When they go to church, for example, she compares Abuela to the explorer Captain Cousteau, trying to make sense of a new underwater world. When Abuela has trouble finding her seat, Constancia then ignores her because she is overwhelmed with embarrassment.

After they return home, Abuela tells Constancia how she felt when Constancia failed to help her: "You made me feel like a zero, like a nothing" (paragraph 16). Her feelings of worthlessness are shown through this smile, a comparison that would include the words "like" or "as." "Zero" is also used in the story's title "Abuela Invents the Zero." It shows how important this simile is. It suggests that Constancia do not realize how much neglect can hurt another person until this is explained by her grandmother. So see how Abuela's simile shows the need to help relatives find ways to be a part of a community, even if that community is unfamiliar to them.

~~In conclusion, metaphor is used in *The House on Mango Street*, "Slam, Dunk, & Hook," and "Abuela Invents the Zero" to show different ideas about people and their communities. Esperanza shows how difficult it is when you have trouble fitting into a community, while strength in community bonds is found by the~~

Skill:
Transitions

Donovan strengthens the cohesion between these paragraphs by starting the topic sentence with the phrase "As a contrast." This transition shows readers that the third body paragraph will include reasons and evidence that significantly differ from the reasons and evidence that Donovan presented in the second body paragraph. However, both of these paragraphs still work together to support his claim.

Please note that excerpts and passages in the StudySync® library and this workbook are intended as touchstones to generate interest in an author's work. The excerpts and passages do not substitute for the reading of entire texts, and StudySync® strongly recommends that students seek out and purchase the whole literary or informational work in order to experience it as the author intended. Links to online resellers are available in our digital library. In addition, complete works may be ordered through an authorized reseller by filling out and returning to StudySync® the order form enclosed in this workbook.

Reading & Writing Companion   105

NOTES

Skill:
Conclusions

Donovan revises his conclusion to make it clearer and more engaging. Rather than repeating his thesis statement in the same words that he used in the introduction, Donovan decides to rephrase it. The rephrased thesis statement at the beginning of the conclusion shows how Donovan's argument has evolved over the course of the essay.

~~speaker in the poem. Under different circumstances, Constancia abandons her grandmother when she is lost in "Abuela Invents the Zero," and Abuela uses the number zero as a metaphor to explain how that disrespect makes her feel.~~

The *House on Mango Street*, "Slam, Dunk, & Hook," and "Abuela Invents the Zero" each use metaphor to show readers how community can effect a person's identity. In *The House on Mango Street*, Esperanza's name reveals a longing to feel like she belongs in her community. The speaker in "Slam, Dunk, & Hook" also offers a different perspective by using metaphors to illustrate how a person can find strength in community bonds. Under different circumstances, Constancia abandons her grandmother when she is lost in "Abuela Invents the Zero," and Abuela uses the number zero as a metaphor to explain how that disrespect made her feel. In each text, figurative language helps readers understand how a community can influence the way people see themselves.

Skill:
Introductions

••• CHECKLIST FOR INTRODUCTIONS

Before you write your introduction, ask yourself the following questions:

- What is my claim? Have I recognized opposing claims that disagree with mine or use a different perspective? How can I use them to make my own claim more unique and specific?

- How can I introduce my topic clearly?

- How will your "hook" grab your readers' interest? You might:

  > start with an attention-grabbing statement

  > begin with an intriguing question

  > use descriptive words to set a scene

Below are two strategies to help you introduce your claim and topic clearly in an introduction:

- Peer Discussion

  > Discuss your thesis statement and plan for supporting it with a partner.

  > Discuss claims that disagree with yours and how your claim is different from other claims on your topic.

  > Review your thesis statement and consider revising it based on your discussion.

  > Write ways you can introduce your thesis statement.

  > Write a possible "hook."

  > You may also add a counterclaim and address it.

- Freewriting

  > Freewrite for ten minutes about your topic. Don't worry about grammar, punctuation, or having fully formed ideas. The point of freewriting is to discover ideas.

  > Review your thesis statement and consider revising it based on ideas you have discovered.

  > Write ways you can introduce your thesis statement.

  > Write a possible "hook."

  > You may also add a counterclaim and address it.

↻ YOUR TURN

Choose the best answer to each question.

1. Below is Donovan's introduction from a previous draft. Donovan would like to add a sentence to grab his readers' attention. Which sentence could he add before sentence 1 to help achieve this goal?

> (1) It is not easy to capture someone's identity in a limited number of words. (2) However, authors often use figurative language, such as metaphor, to reveal characters' qualities and experiences in unique ways. (3) Authors can use metaphor to show why it is important to be part of a community.

- ○ A. How can you ever really understand another person?
- ○ B. Metaphors are comparisons between two seemingly unlike things.
- ○ C. Identity refers to all of the qualities that make someone who they are.
- ○ D. Being part of a community is an important aspect of identity.

2. Below is the introduction from a previous draft of Donovan's essay. Donovan would like to preview the main ideas that follow in his essay by revising sentence 3. Which of the following revisions will achieve that goal?

> (1) It is not easy to capture someone's identity in a limited number of words. (2) However, authors often use figurative language, such as metaphor, to reveal characters' qualities and experiences in unique ways. (3) *The House on Mango Street*, "Slam, Dunk, & Hook," and "Abuela Invents the Zero" use metaphor to show why it is important to be part of a community.

- ○ A. In texts like *The House on Mango Street*, Esperanza uses her name as a way to express her identity, and that kind of metaphor shows why it is important to be a part of the community.
- ○ B. In fiction and poetry, authors use metaphor to show why it is important to be part of a community.
- ○ C. While some may argue that metaphors are not useful, authors can use metaphor to show why it is important to be part of a community.
- ○ D. No change needs to be made to this sentence.

✎ WRITE

Use the steps in the checklist section to revise the introduction of your literary analysis.

Skill: Transitions

••• CHECKLIST FOR TRANSITIONS

Before you revise your current draft to include transitions, think about:

- the key ideas you discuss in your body paragraphs
- how your paragraphs connect together to support your claim(s)
- the relationships among your claim(s), reasons, and evidence
- the logical progression of your argument

Next, reread your current draft and note areas in your essay where:

- the relationships between your claim(s) and the reasons and evidence are unclear, identifying places where you could add linking words or other transitional devices to make your argument more cohesive. Look for:

  > sudden jumps in your ideas

  > breaks between paragraphs where the ideas in the next paragraph are not logically following from the previous one

Revise your draft to use words, phrases, and clauses to create cohesion and clarify the relationships among claim(s) and reasons, using the following questions as a guide:

- Are there unifying relationships between the claims, reasons, and evidence I present in my argument?
- Have I clarified, or made clear, these relationships?
- What linking words (such as conjunctions), phrases, or clauses could I add to my argument to clarify the relationships between the claims, reasons, and evidence I present?

↻ YOUR TURN

Choose the best answer to each question.

1. Below is a body paragraph from a previous draft of Donovan's literary analysis. Donovan notices a sudden jump in ideas at the beginning of the second paragraph in this excerpt. Which of the following could replace the underlined sentence in this body paragraph and provide the most effective transition to the ideas that follow?

> The metaphors in these texts help readers understand why it is important to be part of a community.
>
> <u>At the beginning of *The House on Mango Street,* Esperanza does not like any of the places where she has lived.</u> She describes the condition of one small apartment that a nun from her school saw: "the third floor, the paint peeling, wooden bars Papa had nailed on the windows so we wouldn't fall out" (paragraph 7). She is ashamed of these conditions, and she wants to show other people a home that makes her proud.

- ○ A. At the beginning of *The House on Mango Street*, Esperanza does not think that she can be a part of her community because she is not proud of where she lives.
- ○ B. At the beginning of *The House on Mango Street*, Esperanza focuses on her home and why she is ashamed of it.
- ○ C. At the beginning of *The House on Mango Street*, Esperanza does not live in a house even though houses become a metaphor in this story.
- ○ D. At the beginning of *The House on Mango Street*, Esperanza needs to find a way to feel proud of herself and her community.

2. Below is a body paragraph from a previous draft of Donovan's literary analysis. Donovan would like to add a transition word or phrase to help readers move from sentence 4 to sentence 5. Which transition will work best?

(1) In "Slam, Dunk, & Hook," a game of basketball is used as a metaphor for a strong and supportive community. (2) Throughout the poem, the narrator uses the first-person plural to describe his friends' perspective as a whole, rather than his own. (3) This point of view emphasizes that they all share the amazing experience that he describes. (4) When these friends play together, they surpass what they can do on their own. (5) The narrator says, "Lay ups. Fast breaks. / We had moves we didn't know / We had. Our bodies spun / On swivels of bone & faith, / Through a lyric slipknot / Of joy" (lines 34–39).

○ A. Similarly,
○ B. For example,
○ C. In addition to that detail,
○ D. As a result,

✏ WRITE

Use the questions in the checklist section to revise one of your body paragraphs. Look for a variety of ways to use words, phrases, and clauses to create cohesion and clarify the relationships among ideas in this section. Those ideas may include your claim, counterclaims, reasons, and evidence.

Please note that excerpts and passages in the StudySync® library and this workbook are intended as touchstones to generate interest in an author's work. The excerpts and passages do not substitute for the reading of entire texts, and StudySync® strongly recommends that students seek out and purchase the whole literary or informational work in order to experience it as the author intended. Links to online resellers are available in our digital library. In addition, complete works may be ordered through an authorized reseller by filling out and returning to StudySync® the order form enclosed in this workbook.

Reading & Writing
Companion

111

Skill:
Style

••• CHECKLIST FOR STYLE

First, reread the draft of your argumentative essay and identify the following:

- places where you use slang, contractions, abbreviations, and a conversational tone
- areas where you could use subject-specific or academic language in order to help persuade or inform your readers
- moments where you use first person (*I*) or second person (*you*)
- areas where sentence structure lacks variety
- incorrect uses of the conventions of standard English for grammar, spelling, capitalization, and punctuation

Establish and maintain a formal style in your essay, using the following questions as a guide:

- Have I avoided slang in favor of academic language?
- Did I consistently use a third-person point of view, using third-person pronouns (*he, she, they*)?
- Have I varied my sentence structure and the length of my sentences? Apply these specific questions where appropriate:

  > Where should I make some sentences longer by using conjunctions to connect independent clauses, dependent clauses, and phrases?

  > Where should I make some sentences shorter by separating any independent clauses?

- Did I follow the conventions of standard English, including:

  > grammar?

  > spelling?

  > capitalization?

  > punctuation?

⟳ YOUR TURN

Choose the best answer to each question.

1. Below is a section from a previous draft of Donovan's literary analysis. He sees that he needs to make sentence 2 shorter by dividing it into independent clauses that are written in a formal style. Which revision successfully divides the sentence into independent clauses that are written in a formal style?

> (1) The speaker in the poem "Slam, Dunk, & Hook" has found a way to connect with a group of friends who play basketball. (2) The poet emphasizes that he and his friends are interconnected by using first-person plural pronouns like *we* and *us* instead of *I*, and he uses the metaphor of a labyrinth to show how his friends feel when they play basketball together. (3) He says, "In the roundhouse / Labyrinth our bodies / Created, we could almost / Last forever, poised in midair / Like storybook sea monsters."

- ○ A. The poet emphasizes that he and his friends are interconnected. He uses first-person plural pronouns like *we* and *us* instead of *I*. He uses the metaphor of a labyrinth to show how his friends feel when they play basketball together.

- ○ B. By using first-person plural pronouns like *we* and *us* instead of *I*, the poet emphasizes that he and his friends are interconnected. And he uses the metaphor of a labyrinth to show how his friends feel when they play basketball together.

- ○ C. The poet emphasizes that he and his friends are interconnected by using first-person plural pronouns like *we* and *us* instead of *I*. He also uses the metaphor of a labyrinth to show how his friends feel when they play basketball together.

- ○ D. The poet emphasizes that he and his friends are interconnected by using first-person plural pronouns like *we* and *us* instead of *I* and the metaphor of a labyrinth. This shows how his friends feel when they play basketball together.

Please note that excerpts and passages in the StudySync® library and this workbook are intended as touchstones to generate interest in an author's work. The excerpts and passages do not substitute for the reading of entire texts, and StudySync® strongly recommends that students seek out and purchase the whole literary or informational work in order to experience it as the author intended. Links to online resellers are available in our digital library. In addition, complete works may be ordered through an authorized reseller by filling out and returning to StudySync® the order form enclosed in this workbook.

Reading & Writing
Companion

113

2. Below is a section from a previous draft of Donovan's literary analysis. Donovan wants to add a sentence after the quotation in sentence 3 to explain why that textual evidence is important. Based on the checklist, which version of his sentence works best?

(1) The speaker in the poem "Slam, Dunk, & Hook" has found a way to connect with a group of friends who play basketball. (2) The poet emphasizes that he and his friends are interconnected by using first-person plural pronouns like *we* and *us* instead of *I*, and he uses the metaphor of a labyrinth to show how his friends feel when they play basketball together. (3) He says, "In the roundhouse / Labyrinth our bodies / Created, we could almost / Last forever, poised in midair / Like storybook sea monsters."

○ A. Each basketball player in this group gets more power and skills when they play together, so they are an example of a strong community.

○ B. This group of friends shows you an example of a strong community because they gain power and skills from their connection to one another.

○ C. When they're playing basketball together, they're power and skills increase.

○ D. The labyrinth is a metaphor for a strong community that gives every member more power and skills than they could have on their own.

✎ WRITE

Use the steps in the checklist section to add to or revise the language of one paragraph from your draft by establishing and maintaining a formal style.

Skill: Conclusions

••• CHECKLIST FOR CONCLUSIONS

Before you write your conclusion, ask yourself the following questions:

- How can I rephrase the thesis statement in my concluding section or statement? What impression can I make on my reader?

- How can I write my conclusion so that it supports and follows logically from my argument?

- Should I include a call to action?

- How can I conclude with a memorable comment?

Below are two strategies to help you provide a concluding statement or section that follows from and supports the argument presented:

- Peer Discussion

  > After you have written your introduction and body paragraphs, talk with a partner and tell him or her what you want readers to remember, writing notes about your discussion.

  > Review your notes and think about what you wish to express in your conclusion.

  > Do not simply repeat your claim or thesis statement. Rephrase your main idea to show the depth of your knowledge, convey the importance of your idea, and encourage readers to adopt your view.

  > Write your conclusion.

- Freewriting

  > Freewrite for ten minutes about what you might include in your conclusion. Don't worry about grammar, punctuation, or having fully formed ideas. The point of freewriting is to discover ideas.

  > Review your notes and think about what you wish to express in your conclusion.

  > Do not simply repeat your claim or thesis statement. Rephrase your main idea to show the depth of your knowledge, support for your argument, and the importance of your idea, and to encourage readers to adopt your view.

  > Write your conclusion.

⟳ YOUR TURN

Choose the best answer to each question.

1. Below is the conclusion from Donovan's first draft. Donovan's peer said that he needed to show readers that the conclusion supports and follows logically from his argument. What is an effective way to do that?

> The saying "a picture is worth one thousand words" is challenged by the authors of these three texts. That is because they use figurative language to reveal who these characters are and how they relate to their communities. So no selfies are needed to help readers understand these individuals—just similes and metaphors.

○ A. Make the style of the language more formal.

○ B. Summarize the evidence that supports this claim and show how it is connected to the claim.

○ C. Define the terms *figurative language*, *simile*, and *metaphor* for readers.

○ D. Add a transition word, phrase, or clause that shows how this paragraph relates to the one that precedes it.

2. Below is the conclusion from a later draft of Donovan's essay. Donovan would like to add a sentence to bring his essay to a more effective close. Which sentence could he add after sentence 4 to help achieve this goal?

(1) Authors of all three stories use metaphor to teach readers how belonging to a community can affect a person's identity. (2) Esperanza's experience in *The House on Mango Street* shows how hard it is when you have trouble fitting into a community. (3) The speaker's experiences in "Slam, Dunk, & Hook" show how a person can find strength in being a part of a community. (4) The conflict between Constancia and her grandmother in "Abuela Invents the Zero" shows how painful it is to be rejected, especially by someone you love.

○ A. How would you respond to being rejected by someone you love?

○ B. Each of these characters is brave for overcoming challenges and showing leadership despite their fear, which is not an easy thing for most people, including me, to do.

○ C. Even though each of these individuals has a unique identity, the figurative language used to tell their stories makes their experiences more relatable to the reader.

○ D. The title of each story is important in relaying themes to the reader.

✏ WRITE

Use the questions in the checklist section to revise the conclusion of your literary analysis.

Literary Analysis Writing Process: Revise

PLAN	DRAFT	REVISE	EDIT AND PUBLISH

You have written a draft of your literary analysis. You have also received input from your peers about how to improve it. Now you are going to revise your draft.

← REVISION GUIDE

Examine your draft to find areas for revision. Keep in mind your purpose and audience as you revise for clarity, development, organization, and style. Use the guide below to help you review:

Review	Revise	Example
Clarity		
Reread your literary analysis and see if each idea flows into the next idea. Annotate places where the connection between ideas is not clear.	Focus on a paragraph that has the most annotations. Then, revise that section by using words, phrases, and clauses to clarify relationships among your claim, counterclaims, reasons, and evidence.	In this excerpt, ~~She~~ she even wants to change her name to solve the problem. As a result, ~~Her~~ her name acts as a metaphor, and ~~It~~ it holds more than one meaning in this selection.
Development		
Identify each claim in your literary analysis. Annotate any places where a reason does not clearly support a claim or where evidence does not clearly support a reason.	Focus on a single place where a reason or evidence does not clearly support a claim. Then, revise that section by adding a reason or textual evidence that clearly supports the claim.	In the poem, the speaker and his friends create a strong community based on basketball. In fact, ~~The~~ the speaker even ~~uses~~ speaks on behalf of the group by using the pronouns *we* and *our* instead of *I* throughout the poem. These pronouns emphasize that the speaker is describing experiences he has shared with his friends.

Review	Revise	Example
Organization		
Reread your thesis statement, and annotate any parts of the statement that need to be updated to reflect discoveries that you made while you were writing your draft or the revisions that you have made so far.	Use the annotations that you have made to revise your thesis statement. Your revised statement should include any updated claims and let readers anticipate how you have supported them in the body of your literary analysis.	Each one of these metaphors ~~shows not only who the characters are, but why it is important to be part of a community.~~ helps readers see how a character's community can influence his or her identity.
Style: Word Choice		
Identify sentences that have a conversational style, and replace those with sentences that have a formal style.	Select one to two sentences to rewrite by using a formal style.	. . .~~Like my name,~~ Esperanza's name is a major part of her identity, so she feels out of place when her classmates ~~can't say~~ struggle with it.
Style: Sentence Variety		
Read your literary analysis aloud. Annotate places where there are too many long sentences or short sentences in a row. Take note of long sentences and short sentences that are hard to follow as well.	Select one long sentence to revise or a set of shorter sentences to combine.	Under different circumstances, Constancia abandons her grandmother when she is lost in "Abuela Invents the Zero~~,~~." ~~and~~ Abuela then uses the number zero as a metaphor to explain how that disrespect made her feel.

✏ WRITE

Use the guide above, as well as your peer reviews, to help you evaluate your literary analysis to determine areas that should be revised.

Grammar:
Active and Passive Voice

Active and Passive Voice

Generally speaking, the active voice makes a stronger impression than the passive voice. It helps make writing clearer for readers. In good writing, most sentences will use the active voice.

Voice	Text
Active	**The passengers in their cabins felt** the jar too, and tried to connect it with something familiar. *A Night to Remember*
Active	**Her husband drew the talisman** from his pocket, and then all three burst into laughter as the sergeant-major, with a look of alarm on his face, caught him by the arm. "The Monkey's Paw"

However, the passive voice is useful when the "doer" of an action is unknown or if it is less important than the action or the object. To form the passive voice, use a form of the auxiliary verb *be* with the past participle of the verb. The tense of the auxiliary verb determines the tense of the passive verb.

Voice	Sentence
Passive	A war cabinet **has been formed** of five members, representing, with the Labour, Opposition, and Liberals, the unity of the nation. *Blood, Toil, Tears and Sweat*
Passive	At last the question of my sanity or insanity **was to be decided**. *Ten Days in a Mad-House*

⟳ YOUR TURN

1. Read the sentence below. Then pick the version that correctly changes it to the active voice.

> The heavens were studied by ancient astronomers.

  ○ A. Ancient astronomers studied the heavens.
  ○ B. The heavens would have been studied by ancient astronomers.
  ○ C. The heavens were of interest to ancient astronomers.
  ○ D. No change needs to be made to this sentence.

2. Read the sentence below. Then pick the version that correctly changes it to the passive voice.

> Hipparchus established an observatory in the third century BCE.

  ○ A. In the third century BCE, Hipparchus established an observatory.
  ○ B. Hipparchus will establish an observatory in the third century BCE.
  ○ C. An observatory was established by Hipparchus in the third century BCE.
  ○ D. No change needs to be made to this sentence.

3. Read the sentence below. Then pick the version that correctly changes it to the active voice.

> A solar eclipse was predicted by Thales of Miletus in 585 BCE.

  ○ A. A solar eclipse has been predicted by Thales of Miletus in 585 BCE.
  ○ B. Thales of Miletus predicted a solar eclipse in 585 BCE.
  ○ C. Miletus was the place where a solar eclipse was predicted by Thales in 585 BCE.
  ○ D. No change needs to be made to this sentence.

4. Read the sentence below. Then pick the version that correctly changes it to the passive voice.

> In 1543, Copernicus, a Polish astronomer, suggested the theory that the earth orbits the sun.

  ○ A. In 1543, the theory that the earth orbits the sun was suggested by Copernicus, a Polish astronomer.
  ○ B. Copernicus, a Polish astronomer, suggested the theory that the earth orbits the sun in 1543.
  ○ C. A Polish astronomer, Copernicus, suggested the theory that the earth orbits the sun in 1543.
  ○ D. No change needs to be made to this sentence.

Grammar:
Verb Moods

Mood can be indicative, imperative, interrogative, or subjunctive. Of these four, the indicative will make up the majority of a written work. However, because the subjunctive is the least used, it is the easiest to get wrong, so familiarize yourself with this mood to avoid problems.

Mood	Text
Indicative	Inside the floating cloak he was tall, thin, and bony; and his hair was red beneath the black cap. *Lord of the Flies*
Imperative	"Go and get it and wish," cried his wife, quivering with excitement. *"The Monkey's Paw"*
Interrogative	Will the murderers break and give themselves away? When the victim does not show up for the party will his father suspect? *Let 'Em Play God*
Subjunctive	"You know the Queen of England, if she were here, would have to lift her veil," he said, very kindly. *Ten Days in a Mad-House*

🔁 YOUR TURN

1. This sentence is indicative. How could this be rewritten to make it interrogative?

> When you get home, I'd appreciate it if you'd let the dog out.

○ A. When you get home, let the dog out.
○ B. When you get home, could you let the dog out?
○ C. When you get home, please let the dog out.
○ D. No change needs to be made to this sentence.

2. This sentence is imperative. How could this be rewritten to make it indicative?

> Mow the lawn this weekend.

○ A. Don't forget to mow the lawn.
○ B. This weekend, mow the lawn.
○ C. You need to mow the lawn this weekend.
○ D. No change needs to be made to this sentence.

3. This sentence is in the subjunctive. How could this be rewritten to make it indicative?

> I wish there were more people signed up for the lecture series.

○ A. I wish there was more people signed up for the lecture series.
○ B. We need to have more people signed up for the lecture series.
○ C. If I were planning a lecture series, I would want more people to sign up.
○ D. No change needs to be made to this sentence.

4. This sentence is indicative. How could this be rewritten to make it subjunctive?

> They will serve roast chicken at the dinner this evening.

○ A. I recommend that roast chicken be served at the dinner this evening.
○ B. Will roast chicken be served at the dinner this evening?
○ C. They are serving dinner this evening, and it might be chicken.
○ D. No change needs to be made to this sentence.

Grammar: Consistent Verb Voice and Mood

Voice

Voice is either active or passive. A consistent voice makes writing better and stronger. Though consistency is possible with the passive voice, and the passive voice is sometimes needed, the active voice is more common.

Mood

Mood can be indicative, imperative, interrogative, or subjunctive. Of these four, the indicative will make up the majority of a written work.

Correct	Incorrect
We are going to the store, and we are leaving now.	We are going to the store, and leave now. (The indicative shifts to the imperative.)
Get your coat and come with me.	Get your coat and are you coming? (The imperative shifts to the interrogative.)
If I were in charge, then I would make certain things were done correctly.	If I were in charge, then I will make certain things will be done correctly. (The subjunctive shifts to the indicative.)

Rule	Text
Voice should remain consistent within a sentence.	Someone else who had been listening to the brief dialogue here asserted that he had lived south and that my accent was southern, while another officer was positive it was eastern. *Ten Days in a Mad-House*
Mood should remain consistent within a sentence.	In a few minutes it really did seem as if kind spirits had been at work there. *Little Women*

↻ YOUR TURN

1. Decide whether the voice is consistent. If not, pick the change that will make the sentence correct.

> Lions are the top predators in Africa, and gazelles are hunted by them.

- ○ A. Change **Lions are the top predators** to **Africa's top predators are lions**.
- ○ B. Change **gazelles are hunted by them** to **they hunt gazelles**.
- ○ C. Change **gazelles are hunted by them** to **gazelles will be hunted by them**.
- ○ D. No change needs to be made to this sentence.

2. Decide whether the mood is consistent. If not, pick the change that will make the sentence correct.

> Buy tickets for the movie, and will you come with us?

- ○ A. Change **will you come with us?** to **come with us**.
- ○ B. Change **will you come with us?** to **have you come with us?**
- ○ C. Change **Buy tickets for the movie** to **Buy tickets for the show**.
- ○ D. No change needs to be made to this sentence.

3. Decide whether the verb mood is consistent. If not, pick the change that will make the sentence correct.

> If I were more interested in this subject, I will probably do better in this class.

- ○ A. Change **If I were more interested** to **I had been more interested**.
- ○ B. Change **I will probably do better** to **I would probably do better**.
- ○ C. Change **I will probably do better** to **I have done better**.
- ○ D. No change needs to be made to this sentence.

4. Decide whether the voice is consistent. If not, pick the change that will make the sentence correct.

> The state legislature will consider the proposed laws, and then the bill will be voted on.

- ○ A. Change **will consider** to **had considered**.
- ○ B. Change **bill will be voted on** to **bill will have been voted on**.
- ○ C. Change **the bill will be voted on** to **they will vote on the bill**.
- ○ D. No change needs to be made to this sentence.

Literary Analysis Writing Process: Edit and Publish

PLAN	DRAFT	REVISE	EDIT AND PUBLISH

You have revised your literary analysis based on your peer feedback and your own examination.

Now, it is time to edit your literary analysis. When you revised, you focused on the strength of the argument in your literary analysis. You probably looked at the claim in your thesis statement, organization, style, and the cohesion of your ideas. When you edit, you focus on the mechanics of your literary analysis, paying close attention to things like grammar and punctuation.

Use the checklist below to guide you as you edit:

☐ Have I used active and passive voice effectively throughout the literary analysis?

☐ Does each sentence have a consistent verb voice?

☐ Is the mood of each verb correct?

☐ Does each sentence have a consistent verb mood?

☐ Do I have any sentence fragments or run-on sentences?

☐ Have I spelled everything correctly?

Notice some edits Donovan has made:

- Used active voice instead of passive voice to make a statement stronger.

- Corrected a spelling mistake.

- Made verb voice consistent within a sentence.

- Corrected verb mood.

- Made verb mood consistent within a sentence.

After they return home, Abuela tells Constancia how she felt when Constancia failed to help her: "You made me feel like a zero, like a nothing" (paragraph 16). ~~Her feelings of worthlessness are shown through this~~ She uses a ~~smile~~ simile, a comparison that ~~would~~ includes the words "like" or "as," to express her feelings of worthlessness. The "Zero" ~~is also used~~ in the story's title, "Abuela Invents the Zero~~.~~," ~~It~~ also shows how important this simile is. It suggests that Constancia ~~do~~ does not realize how much neglect can hurt another person until ~~this is explained by~~ her grandmother explains it. ~~So see how~~ As a result, Abuela's simile shows the need to help relatives find ways to be a part of a community, even if that community is unfamiliar to them.

✎ WRITE

Use the questions on the previous page, as well as your peer reviews, to help you evaluate your literary analysis to determine areas that need editing. Then edit your literary analysis to correct those errors.

Once you have made all your corrections, you are ready to publish your work. You can distribute your writing to family and friends, hang it on a bulletin board, or post it on your blog. If you publish online, share the link with your family, friends, and classmates.

The Others

FICTION

Introduction

Ace and the Jeans gang seem to spend a lot of time in detention, while members of the Well-Offs are enjoying things like after-school tennis lessons. On the way home one afternoon, Ace and Jonboy discover a viciously beaten Jeans member lying in the bushes. Was a Well-Off to blame? Are they all bad people?

ⓥ VOCABULARY

expensive
costly

assert
to state with confidence

inferior
lower in rank or position; closer to the bottom of the group

ferocious
very violent and fierce

brief
taking a very short time

☰ READ

NOTES

1   The school doors whooshed shut. I heard Jonboy's sigh of relief. We could finally go home. We had been in detention, again. The teachers seemed to like the fancy Well-Offs better. Those were the rich kids with no problems and no detentions, ever. Mr. Wilson ran detention. I think he hated the Jeans.

2   I noticed Madison and Brittany leaving school. They were holding their tennis racquets. They looked like **expensive** fly swatters. The girls had special lessons after school. We got detention. I usually ignored the Well-Off girls. They ignored us. We liked it that way.

3   We headed down the park path. Mom would be mad because of the detention. She wanted me to "better myself." I didn't feel **inferior**. Suddenly I heard Jonboy gasp. Brad was lying half in the bushes. His clothes were soaked in blood. We pulled him onto the grass. He looked badly beaten. His face was bleeding in a hundred places. He had a deep cut on his jaw.

Reading & Writing Companion

4 I touched Brad's arm. He groaned. "I know who did this," I muttered. "It was Jason." He threatened Brad before. He called Brad a lowlife. He said he was "looking at" Tiffany. Tiffany was Jason's girl. Jason's dad was an attorney who had connections in town. Any trouble Jason got into was quickly fixed and forgotten. Jason got away with everything.

5 "What happened?" Madison whimpered. For a **brief** moment I thought Madison would burst into tears. Brittany stood frozen in horror.

6 "Who would do anything like this?"

7 "Jason did this," I **asserted**. "He's a Well-Off just like you."

8 "We are not all like Jason," Madison insisted. "Most of us are nice people. We just come from families who don't worry about money."

9 "Yeah, right," I growled.

10 "Are all you Jeans like Big Bubba?" she demanded. "I bet he has beaten up people who did not deserve it."

11 It was true. Big Bubba was a **ferocious** fighter. He could knock someone down with one blow of his massive fist.

12 Madison looked sad now. "We have problems, too. Money doesn't buy happiness." She looked at me. "Life is hard, Ace. It doesn't matter who you are."

First Read

Read the story. After you read, answer the Think Questions below.

☁ THINK QUESTIONS

1. What are the two groups in the story? What is the difference between them?

    The two groups are _____.

    The difference between them is _____.

2. Who do Ace and Jonboy find? What do they think happened?

    Ace and Jonboy find _____.

    Ace and Jonboy think _____.

3. Who is Big Bubba?

    Big Bubba is _____.

4. Use context to confirm the meaning of the word *brief* as it is used in "The Others." Write your definition of *brief* here.

    Brief means _____.

    A context clue is _____.

5. What is another way to say that something is *inferior*?

    Something is _____.

Please note that excerpts and passages in the StudySync® library and this workbook are intended as touchstones to generate interest in an author's work. The excerpts and passages do not substitute for the reading of entire texts, and StudySync® strongly recommends that students seek out and purchase the whole literary or informational work in order to experience it as the author intended. Links to online resellers are available in our digital library. In addition, complete works may be ordered through an authorized reseller by filling out and returning to StudySync® the order form enclosed in this workbook.

Reading & Writing
Companion

131

Skill:
Analyzing Expressions

★ DEFINE

When you read, you may find English expressions that you do not know. An **expression** is a group of words that communicates an idea. Three types of expressions are idioms, sayings, and figurative language. They can be difficult to understand because the meanings of the words are different from their **literal**, or usual, meanings.

An **idiom** is an expression that is commonly known among a group of people. For example: "It's raining cats and dogs" means it is raining heavily. **Sayings** are short expressions that contain advice or wisdom. For instance: "Don't count your chickens before they hatch" means do not plan on something good happening before it happens. **Figurative** language is when you describe something by comparing it with something else, either directly (using the words *like* or *as*) or indirectly. For example, "I'm as hungry as a horse" means I'm very hungry. None of the expressions are about actual animals.

••• CHECKLIST FOR ANALYZING EXPRESSIONS

To determine the meaning of an expression, remember the following:

✓ If you find a confusing group of words, it may be an expression. The meaning of words in expressions may not be their literal meaning.

- Ask yourself: Is this confusing because the words are new? Or because the words do not make sense together?

✓ Determining the overall meaning may require that you use one or more of the following:

- context clues
- a dictionary or other resource
- teacher or peer support

✓ Highlight important information before and after the expression to look for clues.

YOUR TURN

Read paragraphs 10–12 from "The Others." Then, complete the multiple-choice questions below.

---

from **"The Others"**

"Are all you Jeans like Big Bubba?" she demanded. "I bet he has beaten up people who did not deserve it."

It was true. Big Bubba was a ferocious fighter. He could knock someone down with one blow of his massive fist.

Madison looked sad now. "We have problems, too. Money doesn't buy happiness." She looked at me. "Life is hard, Ace. It doesn't matter who you are."

---

1. In paragraph 12, what is the meaning of the saying "Money doesn't buy happiness"?

    ○ A. Rich people are never happy.

    ○ B. Happiness is too expensive to buy.

    ○ C. Things you buy can make you sad.

    ○ D. Having money doesn't make a person happy.

2. A sentence that best supports the correct answer to question 1 is:

    ○ A. "Big Bubba was a ferocious fighter." (paragraph 11)

    ○ B. "We have problems, too." (paragraph 12)

    ○ C. "She looked at me." (paragraph 12)

    ○ D. "Life is hard, Ace." (paragraph 12)

Please note that excerpts and passages in the StudySync® library and this workbook are intended as touchstones to generate interest in an author's work. The excerpts and passages do not substitute for the reading of entire texts, and StudySync® strongly recommends that students seek out and purchase the whole literary or informational work in order to experience it as the author intended. Links to online resellers are available in our digital library. In addition, complete works may be ordered through an authorized reseller by filling out and returning to StudySync® the order form enclosed in this workbook.

Reading & Writing Companion **133**

Skill:
Sharing Information

★ DEFINE

Sharing information involves asking for and giving information. The process of sharing information with other students can help all students learn more and better understand a text or a topic. You can share information when you participate in **brief** discussions or **extended** speaking assignments.

••• CHECKLIST FOR SHARING INFORMATION

When you have to speak for an extended period of time, as in a discussion, you ask for and share information. To ask for and share information, you may use the following sentence frames:

✓ To ask for information:

- What do you think about _____?
- Do you agree that _____?
- What is your understanding of _____?

✓ To give information:

- I think _____
- I agree because _____
- My understanding is _____

↻ YOUR TURN

Watch the "The Outsiders" StudySyncTV episode ▶. After watching, sort the following statements from the episode into the chart below.:

	Statements
A	Even on the inside, you can still feel alone.
B	Both groups are outsiders.
C	Greasers are more emotional.
D	The two groups can connect through their differences.
E	Ponyboy is the first person Cherry has gotten through to.
F	Sharing the meanings of sympathy and empathy.

Information from "The Outsiders"	Shared Information

Please note that excerpts and passages in the StudySync® library and this workbook are intended as touchstones to generate interest in an author's work. The excerpts and passages do not substitute for the reading of entire texts, and StudySync® strongly recommends that students seek out and purchase the whole literary or informational work in order to experience it as the author intended. Links to online resellers are available in our digital library. In addition, complete works may be ordered through an authorized reseller by filling out and returning to StudySync® the order form enclosed in this workbook.

Reading & Writing Companion   **135**

Close Read

✏ WRITE

LITERARY ANALYSIS: The Well-Offs and the Jeans come from two different social classes. However, the two gangs have things in common. How are the Well-Offs and the Jeans similar? Pay attention to the *IE* and *EI* spelling rules as you write.

Use the checklist below to guide you as you write.

☐ Who are the Well-Offs and the Jeans?

☐ How are the social classes of the Well-Offs and the Jeans different?

☐ How are the Well-Offs and the Jeans similar?

Use the sentence frames to organize and write your literary analysis.

The Well-Offs and the Jeans are two _____.

The Well-Offs belong to a social class that is _____.

The Jeans belong to a social class that is _____.

Despite their differences, the Well-Offs and the Jeans are similar because _____

_____.

One detail from the text to support this is _____.

Mom's First Day

FICTION

Introduction

Sometimes life takes you by surprise and challenges you without warning. When this happens, you rely on your values to pull you through. In "Mom's First Day," Yvette is startled when her mother addresses her in a familiar way

V VOCABULARY

hover

to remain floating or suspended in the air

humiliate

to make (someone) feel ashamed or foolish

dressy

formal or elegant in style

tidal wave

a very tall, strong wave that is sometimes dangerous

slump

to sink down or forward

NOTES

≡ READ

1   "Be nice to Mom today," my dad tells me. He sets my sack lunch on the counter. It's not even 7:30 a.m. on Monday and already I'm wishing the week were over. How will I survive a week with my mother as my substitute teacher? "Make her feel welcome," Dad continues. "Remember what school felt like on *your* first day?"

2   Just then my mother enters the kitchen. She looks as nervous as the hummingbird that **hovers** outside the window. To my horror, she is dressed in one of her church outfits: a green silk dress with beige pumps. I am about to tell her she is *way* too **dressy** for school, when I remember my father's words.

3   None of this would be happening if Pepe hadn't been born. Mom used to be a teacher at a private school in town, but she quit during her pregnancy. Now she mostly stays home with Pepe. If I were her, I'd want to get out of the house, too. Don't get me wrong, Pepe is cute, but he cries a lot, and he's usually wet with something.

4   My best friend Katie and I have science class together. We get there early and sit in the back. As the class fills up, I **slump** low in my seat, keeping my head down. Suddenly, everybody gets quiet.

5   I look up. There's my mom, standing in front of the class. She smiles at me, and then introduces herself to the class.

6   To my surprise, Mom does a good job. She even makes the class laugh a few times. But I still can't wait for class to be over.

7   Finally the bell rings. Katie and I jump up. We are almost out the door when I hear her.

8   "Yvette," she says. She's holding my sack lunch. "You forgot your lunch."

9   "Thanks," I mumble. I take it from her without meeting her eyes.

10 "Love you," says Mom, just like she often does, only this time it's in front of my classmates. Everybody freezes. I'm so **humiliated**, all I can do is bury my face in Katie's shoulder. To my relief, the kids around me start to laugh and so I laugh, too. But then I see the sad expression on my mother's face. Her disappointment hits like a **tidal wave**. I don't know what to call this new feeling, but I know I'll be left thinking about it for a long time.

Please note that excerpts and passages in the StudySync® library and this workbook are intended as touchstones to generate interest in an author's work. The excerpts and passages do not substitute for the reading of entire texts, and StudySync® strongly recommends that students seek out and purchase the whole literary or informational work in order to experience it as the author intended. Links to online resellers are available in our digital library. In addition, complete works may be ordered through an authorized reseller by filling out and returning to StudySync® the order form enclosed in this workbook.

Reading & Writing Companion   **139**

First Read

Read the story. After you read, answer the Think Questions below.

☁ THINK QUESTIONS

1. Which three people speak in the story?

   The people that speak are _____.

2. Which class will Yvette's mother teach? Who are two students in this class?

   Yvette's mother will teach _____.

   Two students in the class are _____.

3. At the end of the story, what does Yvette's mother say to Yvette? How does Yvette feel at that moment?

   Yvette's mother says _____.

   Yvette feels _____.

4. Use context to confirm the meaning of the word *dressy* as it is used in "Mom's First Day." Write your definition of *dressy* here.

   Dressy means _____.

   A context clue is _____.

5. What is another way to say that someone is *humiliated*?

   Someone feels _____.

Skill:
Language Structures

★ DEFINE

In every language, there are rules that tell how to **structure** sentences. These rules define the correct order of words. In the English language, for example, a **basic** structure for sentences is subject, verb, and object. Some sentences have more **complicated** structures.

You will encounter both basic and complicated **language structures** in the classroom materials you read. Being familiar with language structures will help you better understand the text.

••• CHECKLIST FOR LANGUAGE STRUCTURES

To improve your comprehension of language structures, do the following:

✓ Monitor your understanding.

- Ask yourself: Why do I not understand this sentence? Is it because I do not understand some of the words? Or is it because I do not understand the way the words are ordered in the sentence?

✓ Break down the sentence into its parts.

- In English, adjectives almost always come before the noun. Example: He had a **big dog.**

  > A **noun** names a person, place, thing, or idea.

  > An **adjective** modifies, or describes, a noun or a pronoun.

  > If there is more than one adjective, they usually appear in the following order separated by a comma: quantity or number, quality or opinion, size, age, shape, color.

    Example: He had a **big, brown dog.**

  > If there is more than one adjective from the same category, include the word *and*.

    Example: He had a **brown and white dog.**

- Ask yourself: What are the nouns in this sentence? What adjectives describe them? In what order are the nouns and adjectives?

✓ Confirm your understanding with a peer or teacher.

Reading & Writing
Companion

⟳ YOUR TURN

Read each sentence in the first column. Then, complete the chart by writing the words and phrases into the "Adjective" and "Noun" columns. The first row has been done as an example.

Sentence	Adjective	Noun
You will complete a group project on conservation.	group	project
Bryan's role was to pick important passages from the text and explain their significance.		
His group asked a few times about his progress.		
Back in science class, Bryan tried to focus.		
Bryan, I gave you that role for a good reason.		

Skill: Drawing Inferences and Conclusions

★ DEFINE

Making **inferences** means connecting your experiences with what you read. Authors do not always tell readers directly everything that takes place in a story or text. You need to use clues to infer, or make a guess about, what is happening. To make an inference, first find facts, details, and examples in the text. Then think about what you already know. Combine the **textual evidence** with your **prior knowledge** to draw a **conclusion** about what the author is trying to communicate.

Making inferences and drawing conclusions can help you better understand what you are reading. It may also help you search for and find the author's message in the text.

••• CHECKLIST FOR DRAWING INFERENCES AND CONCLUSIONS

In order to make inferences and draw conclusions, do the following:

✓ Look for information that is missing from the text or that is not directly stated.

- Ask yourself: What is confusing? What is missing?

✓ Think about what you already know about the topic.

- Ask yourself: Have I had a similar experience in my life? Have I learned about this subject in another class?

✓ Combine clues from the text with prior knowledge to make an inference and draw a conclusion.

- Think: I can conclude _____, because the text says _____, and I know that _____.

✓ Use textual evidence to support your inference and make sure that it is valid.

YOUR TURN

Read the following excerpt from "Mom's First Day." Then, complete the multiple-choice questions below.

---

from "Mom's First Day"

None of this would be happening if Pepe hadn't been born. Mom used to be a teacher at a private school in town, but she quit during her pregnancy. Now she mostly stays home with Pepe. If I were her, I'd want to get out of the house, too. Don't get me wrong, Pepe is cute, but he cries a lot, and he's usually wet with something.

My best friend Katie and I have science class together. We get there early and sit in the back. As the class fills up, I slump low in my seat, keeping my head down. Suddenly, everybody gets quiet.

---

1. At the beginning of this excerpt, Yvette feels:

   ○ A. annoyed by her little brother.
   ○ B. proud to be a big sister.
   ○ C. jealous of her mother's past students.
   ○ D. worried that her mother will criticize her.

2. A detail that best supports this inference is:

   ○ A. "Mom used to be a teacher at a private school in town."
   ○ B. "She quit during her pregnancy."
   ○ C. "Don't get me wrong, Pepe is cute."
   ○ D. "He cries a lot, and he's usually wet with something."

3. Based on details at the end of the excerpt, Yvette:

   ○ A. does not like science class.
   ○ B. is mad at her friend Katie.
   ○ C. tries to avoid her mother.
   ○ D. does not get along with her classmates.

4. A detail that best supports this conclusion is:

   ○ A. "My best friend Katie and I have science class together."
   ○ B. "We get there early."
   ○ C. "I slump low in my seat."
   ○ D. "Everybody gets quiet."

Close Read

✏️ **WRITE**

NARRATIVE: How do you think Yvette's mom feels at the end of the story? Make an inference to decide. Then, write a few sentences from Mom's point of view. Pay attention to verb tenses as you write.

Use the checklist below to guide you as you write.

☐ Who is talking?

☐ What is she thinking and saying?

☐ What happens next?

☐ How does it end?

Use the sentence frames to organize and write your narrative.

Mom was surprised about what Yvette did at the end of class because _____

_____.

Mom thought, "I feel _____

that _____."

At home that night, Mom said, "_____" to Yvette.

Mom hoped that next time Yvette would _____.

PHOTO/IMAGE CREDITS:

studysync

Text Fulfillment Through StudySync

If you are interested in specific titles, please fill out the form below and we will check availability through our partners.

ORDER DETAILS

Date:

TITLE	AUTHOR	Paperback/ Hardcover	Specific Edition *If Applicable*	Quantity

SHIPPING INFORMATION

Contact:

Title:

School/District:

Address Line 1:

Address Line 2:

Zip or Postal Code:

Phone:

Mobile:

Email:

BILLING INFORMATION ☐ SAME AS SHIPPING

Contact:

Title:

School/District:

Address Line 1:

Address Line 2:

Zip or Postal Code:

Phone:

Mobile:

Email:

PAYMENT INFORMATION

☐ CREDIT CARD

Name on Card:

Card Number:

Expiration Date:

Security Code:

☐ PO

Purchase Order Number:

StudySync Text Fulfillment, BookheadEd Learning, LLC
610 Daniel Young Drive | Sonoma, CA 95476